Supplement to the YALE REVIEW, Vol. X, No. 2, August, 1901.

REDEMPTIONERS

AND

INDENTURED SERVANTS

IN THE

COLONY AND COMMONWEALTH

OF

PENNSYLVANIA

BY

KARL FREDERICK GEISER, Ph.D.

Professor of Political Science, Iowa State Normal School. Sometime Assistant in
American History, Yale University.

THE TUTTLE, MOREHOUSE & TAYLOR CO.,
125 TEMPLE STREET, NEW HAVEN, CONN.

PREFACE.

In this monograph the attempt has been made to give a complete and accurate account of the institution of indentured service as it existed in Pennsylvania, in the hope of throwing some new light upon an important phase of our Colonial history upon which comparatively little has been written.

Special acknowledgments are due J. W. Gordon, assistant librarian of the Pennsylvania Historical Society of Philadelphia, for many courtesies, and for assistance in furnishing manuscripts and other material; also to Professor W. G. Sumner of Yale University for important suggestions; and especially to Professor Edward G. Bourne of the same institution for constant aid and direction.

K. F. G.

IOWA STATE NORMAL SCHOOL,
  Cedar Falls, Ia.
    Jan. 28, 1901.

TABLE OF CONTENTS.

CHAPTER I.

INTRODUCTION.

The demand for labor in the American colonies, and the belief that the development of their natural resources by Trading and Land Companies would yield profitable returns, early led to various schemes to promote immigration, and especially to enable the laboring class to overcome the great obstacles to emigration presented by a long and expensive voyage. In England and on the Continent there was an abundant supply of laborers, but the majority of those disposed to seek homes and employment in the colonies were too poor to transport themselves and provide the necessary equipments to battle against the unyielding forces of nature. This drawback was recognized by many of the writers on colonization in the 16th and 17th centuries, and the land companies, interested in the settlement of the colonies, were not long in discovering that in order to populate the country they must devise a system of free transportation by which the poor would be enabled to emigrate. To this the English government readily assented, since, in giving an outlet and employment to the vast army of idle classes that thronged the cities and "threatened to become criminals" if they remained unemployed, it afforded at least a partial solution to one of the great economic problems that confronted her at that time.

Sir George Peckham, a partner in the colonization schemes of Sir Humphrey Gilbert, seems to have been the first to suggest what afterwards developed into the institution indentured service. In his tract on the advantages of colonization, written in 1582, he states "there are at this day great numbers which liue in such penurie & want, as they could be content to hazard their liues, and to serue one yeere for meat, drinke and apparell only, without wages, in hope thereby to amend their estates." [1] By 1619 the system of indentured service was fully developed in Virginia. The later colonies subsequently adopted it with such modifications as were necessary to give it specific form suitable to their conditions. [2] Its history in

---

[1] In Hart; American History told by Contemporaries, I: 157.
[2] J. C. Ballagh, White Servitude in the Colony of Virginia; J. H. U. Historical series; vol. xiii.

Pennsylvania, therefore, does not involve its origin; when that province was founded this institution was understood in all its bearings, the difference here from that of earlier colonies being matters of detail which were regulated by local legislation.

A century after Peckham's work appeared, William Penn proposed a similar, though more elaborate scheme, for the settlement of Pennsylvania.[*] By this time, however, assisted immigration had assumed various forms and had acquired a strong impetus; it was now no longer a question as to the method of transporting the poor classes, but rather what inducements should be offered to settlers on landing. Large tracts of land were offered by Penn to adventurers at prices merely nominal, and fifty acres of land were given for every servant brought into the colony. Similar concessions were made by the proprietors of New Jersey for its settlement; in fact such inducements were offered in nearly all of the early colonies. To advertise the advantages of Pennsylvania over those of other colonies pamphlets and broadsides were issued in various languages and scattered throughout England and the continent, and it is remarkable to what an extent they influenced the tide of immigration.

Generally speaking the indentured servants were those immigrants who, unable to pay their passage, signed a contract, called an indenture, before embarking, in which they agreed with the master or owner of the vessel transporting them, "to serve him or his assigns" a period of years in return for passage to America. The master or owner of the vessel whose servants they thus at once became on arriving in America sold them for their passage to whom he pleased, usually to the highest bidder. The indenture was then transferred to the purchaser who now became the master for the remaining period expressed in the indenture.

In the later history of the institution the term redemptioner becomes common and many modern writers have failed to realize the distinction between redemptioners and indentured servants.

The redemptioner, strictly speaking, was an immigrant, but on embarking agreed with the shipping merchant to be transported without an indenture and without payment of passage, and on landing in America to be given a short period of time in which to find relatives or friends to redeem him by paying his passage. If he were unable to find anyone who would redeem him in the time specified, the captain was at liberty to sell him to the highest bidder in

[*] See appendix X.

payment for his passage, in which case the redemptioner entered into the same legal relation or status as the indentured servant, and was consequently governed by the same laws. Sometimes a redemptioner would pay a part of his passage money on embarking; in such cases, however, the same principle applied as in the case of those who were owing for the entire debt, the purpose of such an arrangement being merely to shorten the time of service.

CHAPTER II.

CAUSES OF IMMIGRATION.

The successive waves of European immigration to the American Colonies can not be attributed to any single cause or to any single set of motives. At different periods different forces are at work, and at any given period various motives impel migration. While one class seeks the virgin soil of the new colonies to escape religious or political oppression, or to better their own condition and provide for their posterity, another class comes to escape the discipline of just laws.[1] The same vessel that brought reckless adventurers, to whom a fruitless search for wealth would signify no loss, also contained those who were leaving comfortable homes, to be disappointed with the pioneer life in the new colony.

But among the varying causes which impelled the population westward, was the constant force arising from the economic conditions of the Old and New Worlds—the demand for labor in the colonies, and the supply of laborers in England and on the continent. On this side of the Atlantic, the virgin soil, practically limitless in extent, the undeveloped mines, the immense forests—all required the application of labor to secure their products and to convert them into forms suitable for trade. In England, during the latter part of the seventeenth century, whether on account of over-population or an ill-adjusted industrial system, there was a large pauper and vagrant class considered a "burden on society." What to do with this class formed one of the great economic problems of the time. In 1697, William III, gave the following instructions to the Board of Trade: "And we do further authorize and require you our said Commissioners or any three or more of you to consider some proper methods for setting on worke and Imploying the Poore of our said Kingdom and making them useful to the publick, And

---

[1] "The great majority of immigrants came from respectable and worthy families, and sought only immunity from wars, and a livelihood for their children; but there were some wild and reckless ones among them—criminals, and fortune seekers. The ministers in their reports complained bitterly of the reckless and. adventurous class from Germany who came to America with runaway schoolmasters and students."—Franz Löher, Geschichte und Zustände der Deutschen in Amerika, p. 76. Cincinnati and Leipzig, 1847.

thereby easing our Subjects of that burthen."[2] There was a constant pressure on the population of England during this period. In Ireland the resources were wasted by the many restrictions placed on Irish industry; tenants were unwilling to improve the land, because if they did, the landlords were likely to raise their rents to the full value of the improvements. "On the whole" says Cunningham,[3] "the condition of population was most miserable." This general discontent among a shifting, surplus population, coupled with the constant demand for labor in the colonies, led not only to a constant, free, and natural immigration, but also to a forced and assisted transportation. What to do with the "idle classes?" how to employ the poor? how induce men to emigrate to America? formed problems for numerous experiments.

In Germany, although the causes were of a different nature from those in England, the supply was no less real and abundant. The claim of Louis XIV, to the Palatinate, which was opposed by the German states in the Triple Alliance under the leadership of William, of Orange, opens a period of devastation to that state, which caused thousands to seek homes in the American colonies. To avenge himself on that Province, and to weaken his enemies, Louis sent an army of 50,000 men, in 1685, to ravage the country; cities and villages were burned; the people were stripped of their possessions, and were forced by the French to plow under their crops; many perished and thousands were made homeless. A few years' immunity from plunder was followed by another invasion of a similar nature in 1693. The outbreak of the War of the Spanish Succession in 1701, the Palatinate being the pathway of the contending armies, added thirteen years more of misery. To all this wretchedness Louis furnished a climax by sending an army into the Province in 1707, to repeat the rapine of former years. This was the beginning of the great German exodus to England and her Colonies,[4] and to the native population which flowed out of Germany at this time, were added many of the French Huguenots, who left their country on account of the persecutions of the King.

When we consider that in addition to the ravages of war, the people in Germany, England, and Ireland, were burdened with heavy taxes, distressed by political, social, and religious factions, it

---

[2] Board of Trade Journals, (Transcripts), X: 236.

[3] Growth of English Industry, etc.: 307. Cambridge, 1892.

[4] Wyoming Historical and Geological Society Publications; Pamphlet by S. H. Cobb. p. 9ff., 1897.

See also S. H. Cobb, The Story of the Palatinio, N. Y., 1897.

is not at all strange that there should be a strong desire on the part of the restless population, to seek homes in a new country, free from wars, from party strife, and social caste. The American Colonies in a large measure were free from these distressing misfortunes, and offered the desired opportunities. The remoteness of the colonies, and the lack of means to reach them, were the chief barriers which interposed. Those who were without the necessary means of transporting themselves and who were assisted in various ways, formed a large proportion of the population in many of the colonies. In Pennsylvania assisted immigration begins with the founding and settling of the colony; its history is concomitant with that of free immigration.[5] Indentured servants are mentioned in the earliest frame of Penn's government, and continue to become a more important class with the increase of population.[6]

The direct causes leading to the settlement of this province were many. To induce immigration, Penn agreed with the adventurers and purchasers, that fifty acres of land should be given for every servant brought into the colony. In a pamphlet published in 1682, his method of attracting settlers is outlined at length. Two classes of immigrants needing assistance are therein recognized: "In the first place there are those who are able to transport themselves and their Families, but are unable to build or stock themselves when they are there; others that have not enough to transport themselves and their Families."[7] As this pamphlet is one of many that were issued from 1682 to the end of the century, to encourage immigration into Pennsylvania, a few extracts will be instructive as showing their general character. The scheme here proposed, is to induce men of wealth to take up large tracts of land, and to encourage those of little or no means to settle thereon for the benefit of the rich. Of the two classes above referred to, "the first of these may be entertained in this manner: Say I have 5000 Acres, I will settle ten Families upon them, in way of Village, and build each an house, * * * * furnish every Family with Stock; * * * * I

---

[5] By free immigration I refer to that in which no conditions were imposed upon the immigrant on account of passage, as for example, future service in the colony.

[6] See Penn's Frame of Government; 1683, sect. xxix. The early laws of New Jersey, likewise recognize servants as a part of the population.

[7] The authorship of this pamphlet is attributed to William Penn, and is entitled "Information and Direction to such Persons as are Inclined to America—More especially those related to the Province of Pennsylvania." Reprint in Penn. Mag. of Hist. and Biog. IV: 337-9.

find them with tools and give each their first ground-Seed. They shall continue seven years or more, as we agree, at half increase, * * * * The charge" of this class, it is stated, "will come to about sixty pounds English for each Family: * * * * The other sort of poor people may be very beneficially transported upon these terms: Say I have 5000 Acres, I should settle as before. I will give to each Family 100 Acres * * * * and thirty pounds English, half in hand and half there, * * * * After four years are expired, in which time they may be easie, and in good condition, they shall each of them pay five pounds, and so yearly forever, as a Fee-farm rent; * * * * In these Families I propose that there be at least two working hands, besides the wife, whether son or servant; and that they oblige what they carry; and for further security, bind themselves as servants for some time, that they will settle the said land accordingly." [*]

In the settlement of New Jersey, as in Pennsylvania, liberal concessions were made to planters and servants. Every freeman embarking with the first Governor was on his arrival provided with a "good musket, with bandeliers and match convenient, and with six months provisions for himself." Also "150 acres of land and the like number for every man-servant or slave brought with him." Seventy-five acres of land were promised to every female over fourteen years of age "and a similar number to every Christian servant at the expiration of his or her term of service." [*] These concessions were made in 1665. In the following year settlers from various towns of Connecticut took advantage of the offer and settled in Newark. Perth Amboy was settled in a similar manner a few years later. To encourage artificers and laborers "that shall transport themselves thither out of England, Scotland and Ireland" the proprietors of East Jersey promised to find "work, provisions and pay," special inducements being given to servants.

The large amount of land thus offered on such seemingly easy terms by the governors and proprietors of the new possessions in America was a strong inducement to draw the depressed and comparatively crowded population of the Old World. To the German peasant supporting a family on a few acres in southern Germany where every foot of soil had to be tilled with the greatest care to meet the actual necessities of life, this area offered flattering

---

[*] Similar inducements were offered to settlers in the New Netherlands. See Fiske, Dutch and Quaker Colonies in America; I: 171.

[*] Collection of New Jersey Histo.:al Society; I: 38.

returns for this labor; to the English tenant whose energies were used to augment the wealth of a lord by whom he was oppressed, without hope of his ever becoming master, this seemed a generous offer; here he was to be on an equality with his fellow-men; the results of his labors were to be his own; no oppressive taxation was to bear him down; here he was to be lord of his own domain. The dark side of colonial life—subduing the forest, the constant fear of savages, the want of facilities incident to a sparse population,—was not represented to them in the mass of literature which advertised the new colonies. For unfavorable reports were carefully suppressed by those whose interests lay in the settlement and growth of the colony.

The plan of settlement having been formulated, a large number of tracts, descriptive and otherwise, were issued, which in a large measure, turned the tide of German immigration, from other colonies into that of Pennsylvania. The chief promoters of this advertising scheme, were William Penn and Benjamin Furly, an English Quaker and merchant at Rotterdam, who was the companion and interpreter of William Penn during the latter's visit to Germany and Holland in 1677. "A Letter from William Penn, Proprietary and Governor of Pennsylvania in America, to the Committee of the Free Society of Traders of that Province, residing in London," published in 1683, was translated into Dutch, German, and French in the following year. In the same year there were added to these issues letters from actual residents of Pennsylvania. "The earliest of these pamphlets seem to have been single sheets, or two leaves quarto." [10] The next important work appeared in 1685, entitled, "Good Order established in Pennsylvania." Its object was to counteract a report which had been circulated in some parts of Germany, to the effect that the new Colony was given up to disorder. Another account, more elaborate, was published at Rotterdam the same year, written by Cornelius Bom, a Dutch baker, who came to Philadelphia at an early date and there plied his trade. [11] Less important accounts of Pennsylvania quickly followed.

To counteract the influence of this literature, which was responded to by so many German yeomen, the authorities, both religious and secular, whose provinces were already reduced in population by the wars of succession, issued numerous edicts which

---

[10] J. F. Sachse, Pennsylvania-German Society, VII: 177.

[11] J. F. Sachse, Penna.-German Soc. VII: p. 178.

native country, it appeared to the Committee, that there were books and papers dispersed in the Palatinate,[18] to encourage them to come to England in order to be sent to Carolina, or other of Her Majesty's Plantations." [19]

"This literature" says Sachse, "did much to influence German emigration to America, and after events showed that the printing press in Germany, was one of the most active factors in bringing about the German settlement of Pennsylvania. When fairly started the effects of this movement became phenomenal." [20] The desire to emigrate grew among the German peasantry, until it assumed such proportions as to cause Holland and Germany to take active measures to check the effluent stream, which threatened to depopulate some of the provinces of Germany; as it threatened to change Pennsylvania into a German colony,[21] it caused alarm in England.

So rapid was immigration into eastern Pennsylvania that in the early part of the 18th century the land in the eastern counties was well occupied, and the stream was now directed to the western counties. In 1727 a society was formed, known as the "The Western Pennsylvania Emigrant Society." It was composed of a number of inhabitants of western Pennsylvania, many of them formerly from different parts of Europe. The object of the society was to furnish immigrants "all the assistance in its power, in procuring employment for them, locating them to the best advantage, according to their different stations, trades or occupations, * * * and rendering them all such service in establishing themselves as they need." [22] The advantages which Pennsylvania offered were pictured by this society in glowing colors. Emigrants from all parts of Europe as well as from various sections of the United States, would here meet with friends and acquaintances, who "would

---

[18] Journals of the Commons; Vol. 16: 597. 7 to 10 Anne.

[19] The Queen's picture was upon these books and the title pages were in letters of gold, from whence they were called "Golden Book." Journal of the Commons; XVI: 597. 7 to 10 Anne. "What further encouraged them to leave their native country, was the ravages the French had made, and the damages the hard frost had done to their vines." Ibid: 597.

[20] J. F. Sachse, Penna.-German Soc., VII: 197-8; 1896. This volume contains an excellent account of the literature used to induce German immigration. Following the account, in the same volume, are 56 "Title pages of books and pamphlets that influenced German Emigration to Pennsylvania," reproduced in fac-simile.

[21] J. F. Sachse, Penna.-German Soc., VII: 198.

[22] Hazard's Register of Penn. I: 24; Jan. 12, 1828.

not be behindhand in offers of kindness and hospitality." The Germans, in particular are informed that there is a large and respectable body of their countrymen settled in this country.

The liberal frame of government, the easy manner in which citizenship might be obtained, and the toleration to all religious orders, were among the strongest incentives inducing immigration to Pennsylvania. Every inhabitant on easy conditions, was to "be capable of electing or being elected representatives of the people in provincial council or general assembly." [22] "You are fixed at the mercy of no Governor that comes to make his fortune great," writes Penn to the earliest colonists ; "you shall be governed by laws of your own making, and live a free, and, if you will, a sober and industrious people. I shall not usurp the rights of any, or oppress his person ; * * * * In short, whatever sober and free men can reasonably desire for the security and improvement of their happiness, I shall heartily comply with." [24] Belief in "the one Almighty and Eternal God" was the only condition in matters of religion ; nor, was any one "compelled at any time to frequent or maintain any religious worship, place or ministry whatever." [25] As late as the Declaration of Independence, Pennsylvania and Delaware, the original domain of William Penn, were the only states in which all Christian sects were on a social and political equality. "As for Pennsylvania" says Fiske, "if there was anything which she stood for in the eyes of the world, it was liberty of conscience. In Voltaire's writings Pennsylvania more than once receives admiring mention as the one favored country in the world where men can be devoutly religious and still refrain from tearing one another to pieces." [26]

To what extent religious toleration was a determining factor in immigration, it is difficult to determine. The economic causes were deep seated and abiding. Considered, however, as a collateral or subsidiary inducement religious toleration was potent in promoting the early settlement of Pennsylvania. In addition to the pamphlets and private letters which made the conditions of the colony well known in Europe, messengers were sent at various times to different towns in Germany bearing the news that Penn's scheme of colonization was successful, and that the province was open to all who refused to conform to the requirements of the orthodox religion as

[22] Hazard's Register of Penn. I: 357; Penn's Laws; sect. II. 1682.
[24] Hazard's Annals of Pennsylvania; p. 502.
[25] Penn's Laws, 1628; sect. 35; Hazard's Register of Pennsylvania; I: 359.
[26] John Fiske, Dutch and Quaker Colonies in America; II: 99, 1899.

established by law.[91] The fact that German emigration proceeded in clearly marked waves according to diverse denominations and sects, beginning with those most persecuted, and thence proceeding to those where the religious restraints in the mother country, were more a matter of annoyance than persecution, sustains the opinion that religious toleration was a prominent factor attracting immigration. In support of this, is the fact that most of the early inhabitants, were bands of religionists, whose peculiar views made life a burden in the old country. In the first year of Pennsylvania's existence 3000 Quakers from England landed in the new colony; in 1685 a company of Mennonites from Germany settled at Germantown; about the same time Labadists from Friesland settled in New Castle County, Delaware, then a part of Pennsylvania; in 1695 a band of Pietists were planted on the banks of the Wissahickon; in 1719 a company of Dunkards settled in Germantown; other religious sects followed, among them the Newborn and Schwenkfelders, closing the list with the large incoming of Moravians in 1735. In no other colony were there such diverse and numerous religious sects; in no other colony was religious toleration so prominent a factor. After these early bands had settled in the various localities, they induced their friends in the old country to join them. In this way distinct settlements grew up in the different counties, preserving the customs and manners which they held at home; this distinction is very noticeable in Pennsylvania at the present time.

Up to the middle of the eighteenth century, those who came to Pennsylvania, were, generally speaking, satisfied with their condition. Aside from the misfortunes of the voyage, there was little that called forth complaint. While the early literature pictured the advantages in the colony to a degree far beyond that usually realized by those who left their native country, the wars in Germany, and the industrial depression in England and Ireland, made the change as a whole desirable. But as the influx steadily increased and added wealth to the colonies, evils crept into the system of transportation, by which many were induced to migrate, who afterwards bitterly complained of the change. The demand for laborers in the colony was unabated; shipping merchants found that the passenger traffic was a profitable business, and used every means to encourage it.

It was at this period that a new factor was added to the forces that impelled the human stream into Pennsylvania. A class of Germans who had lived in Pennsylvania returned to Germany, to per-

---

[91] Pensylvania German Society; VII: 172.

suade their countrymen to go to America. This class, known as
the Neulanders, were in the employ of shipping merchants, and received a commission for everyone that they persuaded to take passage.   Recent investigations have revealed, that the greater part of
modern immigration is induced by steamship lines who have agents
all over Europe persuading men to come to America.   They get a
commission on the number of tickets they sell.   In the German immigration to Pennsylvania a similar system[28] was carried on by the
Neulanders.   It must not, however, be assumed that the present
method carries with it the evils of former years.   Over a century's
progress, with all it implies to every phase of life, stands between
the two systems.   The immigrant who came to Pennsylvania before
the middle of the 18th century, seldom returned.   Many of those
induced by Neulanders, who later regretted the move, came as redemptioners, without means, and were, therefore, compelled to serve
in the colony for a term of years ; others, of moderate means, having
sold their property in Germany, were unable to re-establish themselves in their native country, and had to make the best of a pioneer
life.   During this period, therefore, we find many who complain
bitterly of having been deceived by these agents or Neulanders.
Their method of procedure is described in the German newspapers
of the time ; e. g. the Hallischen Nachrichten of 1769 publishes a letter dated 1768 from Muhlenberg, one of the most prominent and
influential Germans, of his time, in Pennsylvania, in which he warns
his countrymen at some length against the trickery of this class.
"These Neulanders," he writes, "first make themselves acquainted
with certain shipping merchants in Holland, from whom they
obtain besides free passage for themselves, a certain amount for
every family, and each individual, that they bring to the Holland
merchants from Germany.   In order to accomplish their purpose
the more readily, they resort to every conceivable trickery.   They
parade themselves in fine dress, display their watches, and in every
way conduct themselves as men of opulence, in order to inspire the
people with the desire to live in a country of such wealth and
abundance.   They would convince one that there are in America,
none but Elysian fields abounding in products which require no
labor; that the mountains are full of gold and silver, and the wells
and springs gush forth milk and honey; that he goes there as a servant, becomes a lord; as a maid, a gracious lady; as a peasant, a
nobleman; as a commoner or craftsman, a baron.   Law and author-

---

[28] See S. G. Fisher, The Making of Pennsylvania: 104-5; Phila. 1896.

ity, they say, is created by the people and abrogated at their will. Now, as everyone by nature desires to better his condition, who would not wish to go to such a country!" Then after being convinced that their condition would be improved in America, and inspired with a desire to migrate, he says, "Families break up, they convert their possessions into money, pay their debts, and the money that remains, they give for safe keeping to the Neulander, and finally prepare themselves for the long journey." [29]

The class principally affected by these agents was the redemptioner, described in another chapter, who formed a large proportion of the German immigration to Pennsylvania from about 1725 to the end of the century. "The greatest part of the strangers," says Abbé Raynal,[30] "who go over to America under these conditions, would never go on board a ship, if they were not inveigled away. Simple men seduced by these magnificent promises blindly follow these infamous brokers engaged in this scandalous commerce, who deliver them over to factors at Amsterdam, or Rotterdam."

When we consider the conditions of Germany, and the inducements offered in Pennsylvania during this period, it is not at all strange that so many were deceived; nor is it correct to assume that all who came were "simple men." People of every rank and profession were lured away. We find among their numbers, soldiers, scholars, artists and mechanics.[31] It was but natural that those

---

[29] Schlozer, Briefwechsel; erster Theil; Heft IV; 218 et seq. Göttingen, 1777. Ich rede nicht von solchen, die nach Deutschland zurück reisen, ihre Erbschaft zu holen, oder auch für andre hiesige Einwoner Gelder, die sie noch in Deutschland zu fodern haben, zu einzuhandlen, und hier wieder zu verkaufen pflegen: dieses ist ein ordentliches und erlaubtes Gewerbe, welche ich nicht tadele—ibid.

[30] History of the Settlement and Trade of the Europeans in the East and West Indies; VII: 410.

[31] "Frequently letters are entrusted in Pennsylvania and other English colonies, to Neulanders, who return to the old country. When they get to Holland they have these letters opened or they open them themselves, and if anyone has written the truth, his letter is either rewritten so as to suit the purposes of these harpies, or simply destroyed. While in Pennsylvania I heard such men-thieves say that there were Jews enough in Holland ready, and who could perfectly forge any handwriting. They can imitate all characters, marks and tokens so admirably that even those whose handwriting they have imitated must acknowledge it to be their own. By means of such practices they deceive even people who are not credulous, thus playing their nefarious tricks in a covert manner. They say to their confidants that this is the best way to induce people to emigrate."—Mittleberger, Journey to Pennsylvania: 42.

who lived in the provinces most thickly populated, or in those whose
fortunes had been ruined by war—it was here that the Neulander
acted—should desire to rise above their wretched condition.   It was
but natural that the offer of a passage, in return for future service
in a country which offered brilliant prospects, should be accepted;
and, while the literature of the times abounds in condemnation of
this species of traffic, it must be remembered that facilities for con-
veying intelligence were not far advanced, especially in those cantons removed from centers of trade.   The alarming extent and the
manner in which this human traffic was carried on during the middle
of the eighteenth century, is well described by Mittleberger in his
Journey to Pennsylvania.   "These men-thieves" he says, "rob the
princes and lords of their subjects and take them to Rotterdam or
Amsterdam to be sold there.   They receive there from their merchants for every person of ten years and over, three florins or a
ducat; whereas the merchant gets in Philadelphia sixty to eighty
florins for such a person, in proportion as said person has incurred
more or less debt during the voyage.   When such a Neulander has
collected a 'transport' and if it does not suit him to accompany them
to America, he stays behind, passes the winter in Holland or elsewhere; in the spring he obtains again money in advance for emigrants from his merchants, goes to Germany again, pretending that
he came from Pennsylvania with the intention of purchasing all
sorts of merchandise which he is going to take there.   Frequently
the Neulander says that he had received power-of-attorney from
some countrymen or from the authorities of Pennsylvania to obtain
legacies or inheritances for these countrymen; and they would avail
themselves of this good and sure opportunity to take their friends,
brothers, or sisters, or even their parents with them; and it has often
happened that such old people followed them, trusting to the per-
suasion of these Neulanders that they would be better provided
for." [32]

The artful means employed in settling the American colonies,
were not alone confined to the continent.   Before the colony of
Pennsylvania was founded, similar seductive methods were extensively carried on in England, by a class called "spirits."   Many who
came to Virginia and Maryland had been deceived by misrepresentations of the conditions in the colonies by the wily arts of these
secret agents.   So extensively was this deception and kidnapping

---

[32] Mittleberger, Journey to Pennsylvania: 38.   Cf. Abbé Raynal, History,
etc., VII: 410.

practiced, especially in Bristol and London, that the expression "to
spirit away" became common all over England, and conveyed with it'
a mysterious and terrifying significance. Children and adults alike
were lured or forced upon vessels in the harbor, or carried to the
numerous cook shops in the neighborhood of the wharves in the
principal seaports, and here they were kept in close confinement
until sold to merchants or masters of ships which were about to sail
for the colonies. As a result of this spiriting away, frauds became
so common, that in 1664, the committee for Foreign Plantations
decided to interpose. Their action was brought about by a petition
from the English merchants condemning the action of the "spirits"
on the ground that many persons who voluntarily left England for
the colonies and became dissatisfied, pretended that they had been
spirited away against their own wishes. A committee was appointed whose duty it was to register the names and ages of all who
proposed to emigrate to America. But this did not put a stop to
the practice. Ten years after the act became a law, it was stated
that ten thousand persons were annually spirited away from England by kidnappers.[22]

The manner in which this cajolery was practiced is described by
one of its victims, a Peter Williamson, a Scotchman, who wrote an
account of his romantic adventures in Pennsylvania in the middle of
the eighteenth century: "At eight years of age I was playing with
companions on the quay. I was noticed by fellows who belonged
to a vessel in the harbor, engaged, as trade then was, by some of
the *worthy* merchants of the town in that villainous practice, called
kidnapping. I was easily cajoled on board the ship by them where
I was no sooner got than they conducted me between the decks, to
some others they had kidnapped in the same manner. In about six
months time the ship set sail for America. When we arrived in
Philadelphia the captain had soon men enough who came to buy
us. He sold us at sixteen pounds per head. I was sold for seven
years, to one of my own countrymen, a North Briton, who had in
his youth undergone the same fate as myself."[24]

[22] P. A. Bruce, Economic History of Virginia; I: 615 et seq. Referring
to those people of England "who are disgusted with the frowns of fortune
in their native land and those of an enterprising disposition" William Eddis
writes in 1770, "These persons are referred to agents, or crimps, who represent the advantages to be obtained in America, in colors so alluring, that it
is almost impossible to resist their artifices."—Letters from America: 67.

[24] The Life and Adventures of Peter Williamson. Liverpool, 1807.

These were among the chief causes which led to the settlement of Pennsylvania, and which made that province unique among the American colonies. To the majority of immigrants it appeared as "their desired haven." Situated in the midst of the English-American colonies, it was the center of trade; its genial climate was suited to all classes; its varied resources gave employment to every industry; its frame of government gave toleration to all religious sects, and its heterogeneous population gave cast to its later history.

CHAPTER III.

THE NUMBER AND SIGNIFICANCE OF REDEMPTIONERS AND INDENTURED SERVANTS.

The number and significance of redemptioners and indentured servants in the colony and commonwealth of Pennsylvania has been commonly underestimated. Unfortunately there are no statistics covering the whole period of colonial history bearing directly on the number and proportion of this class to the whole population. Obvious reasons at once present themselves for the comparative obscurity of an institution so far reaching in its scope and consequences. In the first place, the term "servant," in the common literature of the times, was applied not only to bound servants but to all who performed menial service, and even to officers of the Crown. Then again, while the system of bound service was in its general aspect an institution, distinct as slavery, in its detail there is no distinct line of legal demarcation which separates it in its mild form from the "hired-servants" system which involved work by the year. On the other hand, its close connection with slavery in some of its phases at least, is shown by the fact that there are many laws common to "slaves and servants." Ordinarily, however, the social condition of servants did not differ materially from that of the ordinary freeman. The service carried no ignominy with it; at the end of his service the Redemptioner enjoyed all the privileges and rights of a free citizen, and while under indenture seems to have been regarded as a laborer at present bound by contract to perform a specified amount of labor in a given time.

It was this fact of social equality which renders the general literature of the times vague for purposes of determining their proportion in the colonial population. Lists of immigrants and registries of Redemptioners so far as available, give us the most accurate idea of the proportion of bound servants to the whole population; yet these must be taken with some reserve; those coming from other provinces would not be given in a list of immigrants; neither does a list give any idea of the number who voluntarily bound themselves—and there were many—after having resided in the

colony a number of years as freemen.[1] But although it is difficult to
give in exact numbers, for the whole period, those bound to service,
there is no lack of evidence to show that this class formed a significant part of the population, in several of the colonies, and especially
in Pennsylvania. The combined evidence of letters, laws, statistics,
newspapers of the time and acts of the Assemblies, gives ample
testimony of the important part played by the servant in the history
of the colony.

Just as the cotton interests in the South demanded with its development an increasing number of slaves, so the agricultural, and
other industries of Pennsylvania seem to have demanded for their
development, laborers bound for a number of years. "The labor
of the plantations," says Franklin in 1759, "is performed chiefly by
indentured servants, brought from Great Britain, Ireland, and Germany; because the high price it bears, cannot be performed any
other way.[2] The Rev. H. M. Muhlenberg who was engaged in
pastoral work in Pennsylvania during the middle of the 18th
century, makes frequent mention in his reports to the church at
Halle, of preaching to congregations largely made up of German
servants. In 1750 he writes, "On the last of April I made a journey
to Lancaster; on my return, May 2, an English judge informed me
that there were in that vicinity, many German servants, both men
and women, and that he hoped I might be able to preach to them."[3]
The importance of this class is further shown in a letter of the president of the Provincial Council to General Shirley complaining of
the enlistment of servants for the Canada expedition of 1756: "I
need not remonstrate to you who is so well acquainted with the
circumstances of this province, and who knows every kind of business here, as well among the Tradesmen and Mechanics as the
Planters and Farmers, is chiefly carried on and supported by the
labor of indentured servants, nor what distress must be brought on
the province in general, if the inhabitants are deprived of the only
means of subsisting their families and contributing their reasonable
quota toward any future expedition his Majesty may set on foot on

---

[1] See J. R. Brackett, "The Negro in Maryland," p. 21.

[2] Quoted in the History of Montgomery County, p. 289. Philadelphia,
1884.

[3] Hallischen Nachrichten, I: 505; reprinted, Allentown, Pa., 1886.

The first schoolmaster in New Jersey, in 1676, was to "do his faithful,
honest, and true Endeavor to teach the children or servants of those as have
subscribed, the reading and writing of English, etc.",—Coll. of N. J. Hist.
Soc. I: 246n. Newark, 1875.

this continent against his enemies." [4] The reply from Shirley that "the officers have assured me that they cannot complete their regiments in time without entertaining indentured servants," [5] is still further evidence of their number and importance in the Colony.

In some of the colonies especially Maryland, there was a more important service than merely performing labor as a means of subsistence, demanded of white servants. This is set forth in a petition before the House of Commons of "divers Merchants, masters of Ships, Planters, and others trading to foreign Plantations." The petitioners insist "that the plantations cannot be maintained without a considerable number of white servants, as well to keep the blacks in subjection as to bear arms in case of invasion." [6] In South Carolina it was likewise feared that the great number of negroes imported into the province might endanger the safety thereof, if speedy care were not taken and encouragement given for the importation of white servants. It was for this reason that New Jersey in 1714 passed an act laying a duty on slaves imported into that province, as well as for the purpose of the "encouragement of white servants and for the better peopling of that country." [7]

There was a continual conflict between the institutions of slavery and indentured service. Though the fear that the blacks might become the predominant race was not so great in Pennsylvania as in some of the neighboring colonies, it was frequently entertained by the colonists. White labor was preferred to negro labor generally, and the chief reason that slavery became the prevailing system in some of the colonies, was, because the service was for life instead of for a limited term of years. Had the term of service been equal, slavery would never have been of so great a consequence, and probably would never have gained a firm footing on American soil.

Indentured servants are mentioned in the earliest documents relating to the history of Pennsylvania. The same is true of New Jersey and many of the other colonies. Nearly all of the first settlers brought with them a number of servants. When William Penn was made proprietary Governor of Pennsylvania in 1681, he agreed with the first adventurers to give 50 acres of land for every servant brought into the colony, the servant to possess the land after the term of indenture had expired. From the original war-

---

[4] Minutes of the Provincial of Penn. VI: 777; Harrisburg, 1851.
[5] Penn. Archives, Sam'l Hazard; II: 578; Phila., 1853.
[6] Journal of the House of Commons, vol. X. Nov. 2, 1691.
[7] Archives of New Jersey; first series; I: 196.

rants[8] of surveys, it appears that whole townships were set apart as "Servants or head-land." The original land records show that 4571¾ acres were surveyed and granted "to sundry servants of the first purchasers and adventurers into Pennsylvania." Allowing fifty acres for each servant, and dividing the whole amount of servant land by the number of acres each servant received, we have about ninety of the first purchasers who received land. The number of so-called "First purchasers" to whom these concessions were exclusively made, was about six hundred. The proportion of bound servants to the first purchasers in Pennsylvania, was, therefore, so far as records show, about one-sixth.[9]

After the first settlements were founded, the proportion of servants seem to have been somewhat larger. In the estimated cost of emigrating to Pennsylvania, as set forth in 1682 in a pamphlet by William Penn, the computation is made on a basis of two servants to a family of five. Accounts of individual settlers, where mention is made of the number brought with them, would indicate that the proportion of servants was much larger. Daniel Pastorius, one of the founders of Germantown, brought with him in a company of nine, four men servants.[10] "The number of servants in Maryland" says Brackett, "seems to have been quite large, some colonists bringing as many as 20 or 30 or more. We hear of one who brought in over 60." [11] The early records of New Jersey show that the pioneer settlers likewise brought with them a large number of servants.[12] From these, and various other sources, it is safe to

---

[8] The warrants were sometimes in the following form: "Whereas, A. B. hath made it appear that he came into this province with the first adventurers a servant to C. D. and hath thereupon requested that we would grant him to take up his portion of the headland, etc." Some contain the words, "In the townships allotted to servants."—History of Chester County, (Pa.): 155. Phila., 1881. See appendix VII.

[9] A list of the first purchasers is given in John Reed's "Explanation of the City and Liberties of Philadelphia." Also in Lawrence Lewis' "Original Land Titles in Philadelphia." Phila., 1880.

[10] Pennypacker, Settlement of Germantown: 82. Phila., 1899.

[11] J. R. Brackett, The Negro in Maryland: 21.

[12] Following are the names of some of the pioneer settlers of Perth Amboy, New Jersey, and the number of servants that each brought: Stephen and Thomas Warne in 1683 brought 11 servants.

Thomas Fullerton and wife in 1684 brought 10 servants.

Robert Fullerton in 1684 brought 9 servants.

David Mudie in 1684 brought 13 servants.

Thomas Gordon in 1684 brought 7 servants.

John Campbell in 1684 brought 11 servants.

John Barclay in 1685 brought 6 servants.

estimate that at least one-third of the early immigrants were servants. This proportion was maintained until in 1708 (circa) the German Palatines came in large numbers. There is little evidence concerning servants from this time to 1727, but their number was probably not very large as the German immigrants up to this date usually possessed sufficient means to pay for their passages. But the year 1728 marks the beginning of an immigration of a large number of redemptioners and indentured servants, and the history of immigration from this time to the end of the century is practically · that of servants under various conditions. The number that arrived in Pennsylvania may, therefore, best be seen by a brief outline of immigration · in general, since their influx during certain periods, was generally speaking, proportional to the whole number of immigrants. These periods may be divided as follows:

First; 1682 to 1708. During this period, Welsh, English, Dutch, and Germans arrive, the Welsh being the most numerous and influential class.

Second; 1708 to 1728.. This period begins with a large influx of Germans from the Palatinate, driven thence by the wars of Louis XIV. They were, as above stated, generally speaking, a well to do class; comparatively few of them were servants.

Third; 1728 to 1804. This, like the second period, is characterized by the large number of Germans, and by an especially large and increasing number of servants. The Germans having established themselves in the new colony, now write to their friends, many of whom are poor, and the latter, to better their condition, leave their homes and sell themselves as servants for a term of years in return for passage to Philadelphia. The Scotch-Irish also began to form settlements in Pennsylvania at the opening of this period, and for a quarter of a century were a considerable part of the immigrants.

CHAPTER IV.

HISTORICAL SKETCH OF IMMIGRATION.

In 1681, a year before William Penn arrived, three ships, two from London and one from Bristol, sailed for Pennsylvania.[1] Their passengers were called "first landers" by those who followed. Within the first year after proper requisites were made for a regular settlement, between twenty and thirty ships with passengers arrived, and according to Proud, the early historian of Pennsylvania, "many of them brought servants." In 1684, the population had increased to 7000; the government was now fully established, Philadelphia laid out, the province divided into six counties and twenty-two townships.[2] With the increase of population came an increase of crime and disorder, not because the character of the citizens had undergone a change, but because England was sending her convicts to the colonies.[3]

The class of indentured servants was not recruited from immigrants alone. The courts of this period and for many years after, frequently sentenced freemen to be sold into servitude for a period of years, in order to liquidate fines or other debts; many sold themselves voluntarily, or were sold for a specified time; orphan children were brought to the court to be "adjudged," there being on one occasion, in the Chester County Court, in 1697, thirty-three whose terms of service were fixed by the court.[4] It was common during the whole colonial period for those who wished to learn a trade to bind themselves as apprentices by indenture. Frequently parents

---

[1] Proud's History of Pennsylvania; I: 193.

[2] In 1699, the population of the Province was 20,000.

[3] "The title of redemptioners was a cloak under which many an evil-doer left his country 'for his country's good' to prey upon the peace-loving community of friends." Scharf and Westcott; Hist. of Phila., 4: 856; Phila., 1884. "There was a popular prejudice against subjecting Christians into slavery or selling them into foreign parts, but Cromwell did not draw any such distinctions. Not only did his agents systematically capture Irish youths and girls for export to the West Indies, but all the garrison who were not killed in the Drogheda Massacre were shipped as slaves to the Barbadoes."—Cunningham. Growth of Eng. Industry and Com. in Mod. Times; 109, Cambridge, 1892.

[4] Hist. of Chester County: 430. Philadelphia, 1881.

bound their children, by the consent of the latter, in return for which they were to be instructed in the rudiments of an education or a trade.[5] Franklin in 1717, says in his autobiography: "My bookish inclination at length determined my father to make me a printer * * * * I stood out sometime, but at last was persuaded, and signed the indenture, when I was yet but twelve years old. I was to serve an apprenticeship till I was twenty-one years of age, only I was to be allowed journeyman's wages during the last year."[6]

"The period from 1702 to 1727," says Rupp,[7] "marks an era in the early German emigration. Between forty and fifty thousand left their native country."[8] In 1708 the first body of Palatines was sent to New-York, upon the charity of the Queen, and planted on the Hudson. During the next thirty years many of them sold their holdings and joined their countrymen in the Province of Pennsylvania. In June, 1709, the number of Palatines that arrived in England was upwards of ten thousand. So great was the influx that it caused great complaint in England, and orders were sent to the agents on the continent to prevent "any more being sent over, till those already come should be provided for and settled."[9] The great majority of those who came to England at this time were without means, and were allowed from the public purse 6d. per day to each Palatine, and briefs were issued to the churches in many parts of the Kingdom calling for offerings for the support of this benevolence.[10] In spite of the efforts put forth by the Queen, for their

---

[5] "Henry Nayl brought a servant boy to Court whose name is Alexander Stewart, whose time the said Nayl had bought of Francis Chadsey, and the said boy consents and agrees to serve the said Henry Nayl one year and a quarter above his time by record, if the said Henry Nayl teach him the trade of Shoemaker; if not the said Nayl to allow the said boy satisfaction for the over plus time as the court shall allow."—Quoted in Hist. of Chester County, 431. Phila., 1881.

"William Cope bought a boy whose name is Thomas Harper, who was adjudged to serve five years and three-quarters, if he be taught to read and write, or else to serve but five years, to him or his assigns."—Ibid.: 430.

[6] Franklin's Autobiography: 36. Phila., 1895.

[7] Collection of Thirty Thousand Names of Immigrants in Pennsylvania, p. 2.

[8] A good account of "The German Exodus to England," in 1709, is given in the Pa. German Society Publication. Vol. VII: 257 et seq., by F. R. Diffenderffer.

[9] Journal, House of Commons. Vol. XVI: 597.

[10] The Palatine or German Immigration to New York.—Pamphlet by S. H. Cobb. P. 11. 1897.

care and settlement, seven thousand, after suffering great privation returned in great despondency to their native country. Ten thousand died for want of sustenance, medical attendance and other causes, before they could be transported to their destination.[11] Of the whole number that landed in England, about two-thirds came to America.

In 1709, Governor Hunter, who succeeded Lovelace in New York, proposed to the Lords of Trade to take the Palatines to New York and employ them in the manufacture of naval stores, tar, pitch, and turpentine, in the pine forests of that Province. The proposition was accepted and at once put into effect. In order to pay the cost of transportation and subsistence, to the amount of ten thousand pounds sterling, a contract was made between the Palatines and the Board of Trade: They were to be fed and clothed by the government and required to work until the expense of transportation and maintenance was repaid. Each man was to receive five pounds, and forty acres of land, at the time of settlement, and was not to leave the place designated by the Governor to be settled, without his consent or fail to labor faithfully. On the 25th of December, over 4000 embarked in ten ships for New York, landing after six months voyage, during which over a third of their number died at sea. This was the largest single emigration to America in the colonial period. Many of the children who were left orphans were apprenticed to citizens of New York and New Jersey.[12] About 1200 were settled on the Livingstone manor where they received harsh treatment and rose repeatedly in revolt. The experiment of developing naval supplies proved a failure which involved the loss of the Governor's own fortune. They were asked to settle for themselves. About a third remained on the manor; the rest moved to the Scholarie Valley in 1712, the place originally designed for them. When they had remained here about ten years, they were required, owing to some defect in their title, either to purchase a new title or be deprived of the land and improvements. This caused many to again seek new quarters. Governor Keith of Pennsylvania, learning of their vicissitudes, invited them to settle in his province, and in the spring of 1723, thirty-three families responded to his welcome by settling in Tulpehocken, about fifteen miles west of Reading; a

[11] I. D. Rupp, Collection, etc.: 5.

[12] The number of children apprenticed by Gov. Hunter from 1710 to 1714 was 75. They were between three and fifteen years of age.—Rupp's Collection, etc.: 445.

few years afterwards others followed them.[18] This incident marks a turning point in the history of New York and Pennsylvania, for it changed the current of immigration from the former to the latter province. Henceforth, to the Palatine mind, New York was a province of cruelty and misfortune. Their harsh treatment at the hands of Governor Hunter in contrast with the privileges and security granted to them by Governor Keith, was made known to their fellow countrymen in Germany and for the next forty years the Palatines avoided New York.[14] Emigration was now organized on a large scale. A committee on transportation was formed at Rotterdam, which now was the chief port as well for the Swiss and French population as for the inhabitants of the Rhine valley; between it and Philadelphia ships plied every summer, with regularity for the next forty years.[15]

On account of persecution and oppression in Switzerland, a large body of Mennonites fled from the Cantons of Zurich, Bern, and Schaffhausen about the year 1672, to Alsace, on the Rhine. Here they remained till in 1708, they emigrated to London and thence to Pennsylvania where they made their home at Germantown. In 1712, they purchased land in the Pequa Valley and there formed the nucleus of a rapidly increasing Swiss, French, and German population, to which there were large accessions in 1711 and 1717.[16]

At this time the number of Swiss and Germans in the colony increased so rapidly that it caused general alarm among the English colonists and led to restrictive measures on the so-called "foreign" immigration. It was feared that Pennsylvania might cease to be

---

[18] I. D. Rupp. Collection of 30,000 names of immigrants in Pa.: 5f.; also S. H. Cobb. The Palatines or Ger. Immi. to N. Y. and Pa., p. 16ff. See also, The Story of the Palatines by the same author.

[14] The Germans, not satisfied with being themselves removed from New York wrote to their relatives and friends, and advised them, if ever they intended to come to America, not to go to New York, where the government had shown itself unequitable. This advice had such influence that the Germans who afterwards went in great numbers to North America, constantly avoided New York and always went to Pennsylvania. It sometimes happened that they were forced to go on board of such ships, as were bound for New York, but they were scarce got ashore, when they hastened on to Pennsylvania, in sight of all the inhabitants of New York."—Peter Kalm, Travels in America, I: 270 ff.

[15] The Palatine or German Immigration to New York and Pa. Pamphlet, S. H. Cobb: p. 29. 1897.

[16] I. D. Rupp, Collection, etc.: 7 ff.

3

a British province. Governor Keith stated to his council "that great numbers of foreigners from Germany, strangers to our language and constitution, * * .* * daily dispersed themselves immediately after landing, without procuring certificates from whence they came or what they are * * * * That this practice might be of very dangerous consequence, since by the same method, any number of foreigners, from any nation whatever, enemies as well as friends, might throw themselves upon us." [17] The subject was discussed in the assembly till finally a bill was passed forbidding foreign immigration altogether.[18] This, however, was vetoed by the Governor on the ground of its cruelty.

To counteract the German element therefore every inducement on the part of England was thrown out to encourage the transportation of English servants to the colonies. Measures were even adopted for transporting convicts, who, like servants, were bound for a term of years, the time of indenture being from seven to fourteen years. In 1718, a statute was passed stating that, "Whereas in many of his Majesties Colonies and Plantations in America there is a great want of servants who by their labor and industry might be the means of improving and making the said Colonies and Plantations more useful to the nation, Be it enacted * * * * that when any persons have been convicted of any offence within the benefit of the clergy before January 20th, 1717, and are liable to be whipped or burnt in the hand * * * * it shall be lawful for the court before whom they are convicted * * * * to order and direct that such offenders * * * * shall be sent to some of the Majesty's Colonies and Plantations in America for the space of seven years. When the penalty for crime is death, they shall be transported for fourteen years." [19] Against this statute, there were strong remonstrances on the part of Pennsylvania. The colony had hitherto been free from this pernicious class, though it was not long before the effect of this law was felt as is shown by the following act of the assembly, dated February 14th, 1729: "All masters of vessels, Merchants or others, who shall import * * * * into any Port or place belonging to this province * * * * any person in the condition of a servant or otherwise * * * * who hath been convicted * * * * shall before the convict be landed, pay

[17] Quoted in I. D. Rupp.—Collection, etc.: 9. See also Hist. of Montgomery Co. (Pa.): 135; Phila., 1884.
[18] The Palatine or German Immigration: 30.
[19] Statutes at Large. V: 174; 4 Geo. I C. 11. Sect. I. London, 1763.

the sum of five pounds and give security of fifty pounds to the Treasurer for his good behavior." [20]

To protect the province further from a non-productive and shiftless class common to many of the colonies, an act was passed in the same session by the Assembly prohibiting the importation of "Old persons, Infants, Maimed, Lunatics, or Vagabonds or Vagrant persons." In case they were imported they were to be brought before the Mayor or Justice of the Peace and examined, and if likely to become a public charge, the master or importer was required to send them back where they came from, or indemnify the inhabitants of the province from any charge that might come or be brought upon them by the presence of such persons.

The agitation and alarm begun in 1717, caused by the constant increase of foreigners in the years following, resulted in more active measures in 1727. The Governor and assembly showed themselves in a complete panic in regard to the influx of the Palatines and other foreigners. [21] A meeting of the council was called in which "The Governor acquainted the board that he had called them together at this time to inform them that there is lately arrived from Holland, a Ship with four hundred Palatines, * * * * and that they will very soon be followed by a much greater number who design to settle in the back parts of the province; and as they transplant themselves without any leave attained from the Crown of Great Britain, and settle themselves upon the Proprietor's untaken up lands without any application to the Proprietor or his Commissioners of property, or to the government in general, it would be highly necessary to concert measures for the peace and security of the province which may be endangered by such numbers of strangers daily poured in, who being ignorant of our Language and Laws, and settling in a body together, make, as it were, a distinct people from his Majesty's Subjects." [22] Masters of vessels importing "foreigners" as they were then called, were now ordered to get permission from the Court of Great Britain to bring them into the colony. And it was further ordered, "that a list shall be taken of the names of all these people, their several occupations, and the place from whence they came, * * * * And further, that a writing be drawn up for them to sign, declaring their Allegiance and Subjection to the King of Great Britain, and Fidelity to the

---

[20] Acts of Assembly of the Province of Pa. p. 159. Phila., 1775.

[21] Scharf and Westcott. Hist. of Phila. I: 203.

[22] Minutes of the Provincial Council of Pa. (Col. Rec.) III: 283.

Proprietary of this province, and that they will demean themselves peaceably towards all his Majesties Subjects, and strictly observe, and conform to the laws of England and of this Government." [22] This act was unique in Colonial legislation and preserved the names of upwards of 30,000 immigrants, the original lists of which may still be found at Harrisburg. [24]

The first body of Palatines that arrived after this act was passed, consisted of about four hundred persons. Only males above the age of sixteen were required to actually take the oath of allegiance. It appears from the records of the Provincial Council that the masters of vessels did not get permission from "the Court of Great Britain" as requested, but instead, merely an "Affidavit signed by the Officers of the Customs" in England.

Not content with the precautionary measures taken by the Assembly in requiring an oath of allegiance, under instructions from the home government, they passed an act in 1729, imposing a duty of twenty shillings on all foreign servants imported into the Province. [23] There are no data showing the exact proportion of indentured servants that arrived at this time, but as this act was passed to arrest the influx of Germans, it is quite evident that the majority were redemptioners. In the newspapers of this time frequent advertisements appear of which the following, in 1728, is a sample: "Lately imported and to be sold cheap, a parcel of likely men and women servants."

During the following year 267 English and Welsh, and 43 Scotch servants arrived. The majority of Germans who came as

[22] Ibid: 283.

[24] They have been collected by I. D. Rupp, and published in a book entitled "A Collection of Thirty Thousand Names of Immigrants in Pennsylvania."

All male persons above the age of 16 subscribed to the following Declaration: "We subscribers, natives and late inhabitants of the Palatine upon the Rhine and places adjacent, having transported ourselves and families into this Province of Pennsylvania, a colony subject to the crown of Great Britain, in hopes and expectation of finding a retreat therein, Do solemnly promise and engage that we will be faithful and bear true allegiance to His present *Majesty, King George the Second,* and His successors, Kings of Great Britain, and will be faithful to the proprietor of this Province; and that we will demean ourselves peacefully to all His said Majesty's Subjects, and strictly observe and conform to the Laws of England and of this Province, to the utmost of our power and the best of our understanding."—Colonial Record, III: 283. Phila., 1852.

[23] Col. Rec. III; 360.

redemptioners were agricultural laborers, and acquired land of their own as soon as their term of service had expired. In 1734 the total number of landholders in Montgomery County was 760 of whom 395 were Germans. However, every occupation was represented by this class. The same vessel that brought the schoolmaster and shoemaker, brought also the minister and the tanner. Out of less than 3000 German Protestant males who arrived in London in 1709, twenty-five different occupations were represented.[26]

From 1730 to 1740 about sixty-five vessels well filled with Germans arrived at Philadelphia. From 1740 to 1755 upwards of one hundred vessels arrived, some of which though small carried 600 passengers.[27] In 1749 immigration was larger than at any time during the colonial period. During this year twenty-five vessels arrived at Philadelphia, landing above 7000 passengers.[28]

---

[26] The total number of males and females that arrived in London in 1709, was 11,294; of the males there were:

Husbandmen,	1838	Limeburners,	8
Bakers,	78	Schoolmasters,	18
Masons,	477	Engravers,	2
Carpenters,	124	Brickmakers,	3
Shoemakers,	68	Silversmiths,	2
Tailors,	99	Smiths,	35
Butchers,	29	Herdsmen,	3
Millers,	45	Blacksmiths,	48
Tanners,	14	Potters,	3
Weavers,	7	Turners,	6
Saddlers,	13	Barbers,	1
Glassblowers,	2	Surgeons,	2
Hatters,	3		

Of the whole number there were 2556 who had families.—Pa. German Soc. VII; 321.

[27] Rupp. Hist. of Northumberland, etc.; 53. Lancaster, 1847.

[28] Letter from Rev. Henry Melchoir Muhlenburg, quoted in Rupp's Hist. of Northumberland, etc. 58. Lancaster, 1847.

The arrivals from Aug. 24th to Nov. 9th, 1749, are as follows:

Aug. 24, 240 passengers.		Sept. 26, 840 passengers.	
Aug. 30, 500	"	Sept. 27, 260	"
Sept. 2, 340	"	Sept. 28, 242	"
Sept. 9, 400,	"	Oct. 2, 249	"
Sept. 11, 299	"	Oct. 7, 450	"
Sept. 14, 333	"	Oct. 10, 250	"
Sept. 15, 930	"	Oct. 17, 480	"
Sept. 19, 372	"	Nov. 9, 77	"
Sept. 25, 240	"		

Rupp's Hist. and Topography of Northumberland, etc. 54. Lancaster, 1847.

The population of Pennsylvania at this time has been variously estimated, the average of which may be placed at 230,000, the Germans constituting about one-half of the population.[29] At the time of the French and Indian War, it was estimated that there were 60,000 imported white servants of the several grades in the Province and sometimes as many as 3000 or 4000 would be enlisted in the quotas of Pennsylvania, Delaware, and New Jersey.[30] These, it must be remembered, were actually under indenture at the time, and formed but a small portion of those who had at some time been bound to service, and were now classed as freemen.[31]

From 1725 to the middle of the century a considerable number of Scotch-Irish arrived who settled chiefly in Dauphin and Cumberland Counties. Many of these also came as servants, for on the 10th of July, 1741, a shipload from Cork is advertised for sale consisting largely of "tradesmen of various sorts."[32] They began to arrive about 1720 and came chiefly from the north of Ireland. Many of them were the descendants of the Irish Protestants who during the reign of Charles I, had by massacres and inhumanity

---

[29] Loeher, Geschichte, etc. 75.
Rush, Manners of the Germans, etc. 5

[30] A reply from the army officers of Pa. to the Assembly concerning complaints of enlistment states, "It is the opinion of this board * * * that as a moderate computation we conceive not less than 60,000 (servants) have been imported into the province within twenty years; the number of men raised here may well be spared."—Col. Rec. IV: 468. Aug. 20, 1740.

[31] In Maryland the census of 1752 gives the following proportion of Freemen, Indentured Servants, and Convicts:

	Free.	Ind. Serv.	Convicts.	Total.
Men,	24508	3576	1507	29141
Women,	23521	1824	386	25731
Boys,	26637	1049	67	27752
Girls,	24141	422	21	24584
Total,	98357	6870	1981	107208

Maryland had a larger number of negro slaves, and consequently not so many indentured servants as Pa.—See E. D. Niell Terra Mariae: 211. Phila., 1867.

[32] "Just arrived from Cork, in the Snow Penguin, Robert Morris, Master; A Parcel of likely Servants, used to country work, as also tradesmen of various sorts, such as taylors, carpenters, coopers, joyners, clothiers, weavers, shoemakers, sawyers, chimney sweepers, gardner, tanner, sadler, baker, nailer, smith, barber, hatter, ropemaker; whose times are to be disposed of by the said Master on board said Snow, lying off against Market-street wharfe, or Edward Bridges at his house (commonly called the Scales) for ready money or the usual credit."—Phila. Gazette. July 16, 1741.

been driven from Ireland in 1641, and many of whom fled into the north of Scotland, whence the north of Ireland had been colonized. It was among this class in Scotland and the north of Ireland that the act of uniformity passed by Parliament in 1662 had met with the greatest opposition. In 1713 the Schism Act under Queen Anne was passed, which deprived Dissenters of the means of educating their children in their own religious beliefs by crushing all Nonconformist schools. These difficulties and the unsettled state of affairs in Europe drove many from their native country. Among those who came to Pennsylvania were genuine Scotch as well as Scotch-Irish.[83] James Logan, Secretary to the Proprietaries, writes in 1729, "It looks as if Ireland is to send all her inhabitants hither, for last week not less than six ships arrived, * * * * The common fear is, that if they continue to come, they will make themselves proprietors of the province. Besides these many convicts are imported hither." [84] On account of frequent disturbances between the governor and the Irish settlers, the proprietaries gave orders in 1750 to their agents to sell no land in York and Lancaster Counties to the Irish, and also to make advantageous offers to encourage the Irish settlers to move to Cumberland county, which afterwards became their chief place of settlement.

Although it had not been found practicable to restrict immigration from the Continent the political influence of the Germans was held in check up to 1731, by withholding from them the right of suffrage. In this year a petition was sent to the Assembly by the Germans inhabiting the county of Philadelphia, wherein they pray "that they may be permitted to enjoy the rights and privileges of English subjects." [85] This right was granted, and by the middle of the century their numbers had increased to such an extent that their political power became a source of annoyance to the English colonists. In a letter of 1747, Governor Thomas says the Germans of Pennsylvania are three-fifths of the population. Franklin, in a letter dated May 9th, 1753, says, "They import many books from Germany, and of the six printing houses in the Province two are entirely German, two half-German and half-English, and but two are entirely English. The signs in our streets have inscriptions in both languages and some places only in German. They begin of late to make their bonds and other legal instruments in their own language, which are

[83] Rupp's Hist. of Dauphin County; 51.

[84] Quoted. Ibid. 52.

[85] Hist. of Montgomery County; 135. Phila., 1884.

allowed good in our courts where the German business so increases
that there is continual need of interpreters, and I suppose in a few
years they will also be necessary in the Assembly to tell one-half of
our legislators what the other half says.   In short, unless the stream
of importation can be turned from this to the other colonies   *   *
*   *   they will soon outnumber us, that all the advantages we
have, will, in my opinion, be not able to preserve our language,
and even our Government will become precarious." [36]

A manuscript pamphlet in the Franklin Library at Philadelphia,
supposed to have been written by Samuel Wharton, shows that the
Germans, in 1755, were becoming independent and that they now
largely controlled the political policy of the colony.   He says they
ally themselves with the Friends, through Sauer, who was an influential publisher of a German newspaper; that they are insolent and
call all those who do not ally with their party, the "Governor's men,"
and that they deem themselves strong enough to make the country
their own.   "Indeed, they come in such force, say upwards of 5000
in the last year, I see not but that they may be able to give us language too, or else, by joining the French eject all English.   That
this may be the case is, too, much feared, for almost to a man they
refused to bear arms in the time of the late war, and they say it is all
one to them which King gets the country, as their estates will be
equally secure.   Indeed, it is clear the French have turned their
hopes upon this great body of Germans." [37]   The fear of an alliance
with the French, which seems to have been shared by a number at
this time, had no foundation in fact, for there is no evidence of any
disloyalty on the part of the Germans at any time during the history
of Pennsylvania, any more than among the English colonists themselves.   But their ever increasing proportion to the whole population gave them at this time a political power which excited the
jealousy of the parties.   They were powerful makeweights in the
political balance and their influence was sought by every party.
This was the significance of the immigrants in the middle of the
century, who left the Rhine for Pennsylvania, the majority of whom
came as redemptioners.   They were, by their industry, the principal
instruments in raising the state to the conditions which made it rank
foremost among the English Colonies. [38]

In 1762 the large number of negroes imported into Pennsylva-

[36] Quoted in Hist. of Montgomery Co. 137. Phila., 1884.
[37] I. D. Rupp, Hist. of Dauphin, Cumberland, etc.; 48. Lancaster, 1848.
[38] Benj. Rush, Manners of German Inhabitants of Pa. Phila., 1875.

nia, brought forth remonstrances, for slave labor was now threatening to drive out or destroy the system of white service. There was also a strong moral sentiment against slavery among the German Friends. As early as 1688 resolutions were passed in a Quaker meeting protesting against slavery—the first official action against the institution in America. In 1758, they voted in their general meeting to excommunicate every member of the society who should persist in keeping slaves.[39] The Assembly passed a law imposing a prohibitory duty on the importation of slaves, which was vetoed by the Crown. "Never before," says Bancroft, "had England pursued the traffic in Negroes with such eager avarice."[40] In some colonies the importation of negroes lessened the transportation of white servants. In Pennsylvania, however, the latter were by far the most numerous and important laborers. Their arrival at Philadelphia from Germany continues to attract attention. A letter from Dr. Muhlenberg of January 7th, 1768, shows that the majority of Germans were servants, and that a greater number arrived than could be readily disposed of. He says, "Last Fall five or six ships filled with Germans arrived at Philadelphia, of which a large portion are still in the vessels, not only because their passage amounted to a large sum, but also on account of a general scarcity of money. They are not sold as readily as they formerly were, and must, therefore, submit to their misery." But in spite of the hardships and delays in finding purchasers they continued to pour into the province in undiminished numbers.

The stream of German immigration for which every inducement had been thrown out during the beginning of the colony had gradually increased so that the newcomers were now unwelcome guests, especially in Philadelphia, but except during short intervals, as, for example, when during the hostilities between France and England, from 1756 to 1761, German emigration to Pennsylvania was entirely suspended, the momentum of the current was now too strong to be turned back or even checked. The famine of 1770, in Germany, induced an unusually large wave to Pennsylvania, which lasted to 1791. During these years twenty-four ships on an average arrived annually at Philadelphia.[41] The Pennsylvania newspapers of this period contain a large number of notices of arrivals and sales of servants. The Pennsylvania Packet has an average of about twenty

[39] Brissot's America I; 232. London, 1794.
[40] Bancroft, Hist. U. S. IV; 421.
[41] Franz Loeher, Geschichte und Zustände, etc: 76.
History of Germany, Wolfgang Menzel; III: 447. London, 1849.

notices of "Runaway Servants," in each issue.[41]   In 1789 the importation of Indentured Servants from Great Britain received a decisive check by an act of Parliament the intent of which was to prevent the indenturing, for transportation to America, of persons who might carry thither the manufacturing skill of Great Britain, but the terms of which were comprehensive enough to embrace laborers of all sorts.   German redemptioners, however, continued to arrive as late as 1831.[42]

Franz Loeher, in his Geschichte und Zustände der Deutschen in Amerika says, "The years in which an especially large number of redemptioners arrived in Pennsylvania, were, 1728, '29, '37, '41, '50, and 1751." All later writers seem to have quoted him, and many seem to have inferred that redemptioners came by periods or in waves.   This is true only to the extent that immigration varied in different periods.   The years mentioned by Loeher, to which may be added 1732 and 1733, witnessed a large foreign immigration, and for this reason were years in which a large number of redemptioners and indentured servants arrived.   But their importation was by no means entirely confined to the years referred to.   Notices of their arrival may be found every year in the newspapers of the time. Thus in the Pensylvania Gazette of January 10th, 1739, we read of a "parcel of likely servants, whose times are to be disposed of, just imported in the ship Apollo." [43]   Generally speaking, the number of bound servants, through extended periods, was proportional to the whole number of immigrants.

The economic forces which gave rise to this species of servitude changed very slowly and were in constant operation from the founding of Pennsylvania until in the middle of the 19th century, the last remnants of the decaying institution disappeared.   From 1682 to

[41] The Packet of Aug. 8th, 1774, contains twenty-one notices of runaways, four of them being convicts.

[42] Hildreth, History of the United States; I: 93.

[43] The number of arrivals according to Rupp. are given below. The arrivals from 1727 to 1738 includes all ages. From 1738 no names appear in the captains' lists, under sixteen years of age.

1727	1214	1736	838
1728	987	1737	1736
1729	735	1738	3025
1730	721	1739	1603
1731	632	1746	1131
1732	2191	1749	7148
1733	1432	1751	3981
1734	388	1755	271
1735	272	1756	109

1708 the proportion of servants to the whole number of immigrants was about one-third; from 1708, with the increase of Germans, to 1728, a period in which they were impelled by the wars of Europe, the proportion of servants increased to about one-half the number of immigrants. From 1728 to the end of the century, the great majority of Germans which constituted the main current of foreigners into Pennsylvania were redemptioners. The Scotch-Irish who formed a considerable portion of the immigrants from the beginning of this period to the middle of the century, came under almost the same force of circumstances as the early Germans, and like them, after they had established themselves invited their friends who were in poor circumstances, and paid their passages, in return for which the immigrants bound themselves. A comparison of statistics, from 1786 to 1804, shows that the proportion of servants to all immigrants was two-thirds for this period of nineteen years.[45] The combined evidence from newspaper notices of arrivals and sales, from court records, from laws, from the number of enlistments in the army,—in short, from every source permitting of an estimate,—indicates that this was approximately the proportion for the entire period.[46]

The beginning of the present century marks the decline of the institution of indentured service. Frequent arrivals of vessels, however, still occur in which the majority of passengers are redemptioners. Robert Sutcliff visiting his brother in Pennsylvania in 1804, says, "I noticed that the two female servants employed in the family, had, both of them been lately hired from on board a vessel lying in the Delaware; and which had recently arrived from Amsterdam with several hundred Germans, men, women and children, of that description of people called, in America, Redemptioners."[47]

---

[45] From the 19th of August, 1786, to December 31st, 1804, 3622 redemptioners registered at Philadelphia. During exactly the same period 5509 foreign immigrants landed in the same city. All foreigners were requested to take the oath of allegiance to the Province and the Crown from 1727 to 1775; and to the State after the Revolution. These names are printed in the Pa. Arch. 2d Series, XVII. All those who came as redemptioners during the latter part of the 18th and the beginning of the 19th century, were required to be registered at Philadelphia. Two MSS. volumes—Registry of Redemptioners—covering this period are in the Library of Hist. Soc. of Pa.

[46] i. e. 1728 to 1804.

[47] Robert Sutcliff, Travels in Some Parts of North America, p. 32. London, 1811.

H. B. Fearon who travelled in America in 1817-18, visited a ship in the Delaware, having redemptioners on board.—Sketches of America: 148.

Though the system is declining, the German redemptioners are mentioned in statutes of Pennsylvania as late as 1818, and the Registry of Redemptioners at Philadelphia shows that the last servant was bound in 1831.[48]

On the 8th of February, 1819, a law was passed, "that no female shall be arrested or imprisoned, for, or by reason of any debt contracted after the passage of this act." With the final abolition of imprisonment for debts the institution of indentured service received its legal death blow, and necessarily died out without any special enactment.

----

[*] The last original entry appearing on the Register is as follows: "Fredericka Witmire, of her own free will bound herself servant to John Seiser of the city of Philadelphia, Tailor, for two Years—at the expiration of the Term to have two complete suits of clothes one whereof to be new. Cons. $40." Dated Nov. 28, 1831.

CHAPTER V.

THE VOYAGE.

The progress made within a century and a half, in transportation on land and sea, has been so marked that to one living in the present age a voyage across the ocean has a meaning entirely different from what it had to those who came as pioneers in colonial days. The rapidity with which vessels now ply between the ports of Europe and America, and the conveniences offered to passengers, have so modified the mode of travel, that it is necessary to be reminded of former conditions in order to understand the significance of a voyage during the period in which the institution of indentured service was in existence. At that time the journey to America was the great bane of the immigrant. It was one of the direct causes of the system of indentured service. The number of passengers that were compelled to sell themselves into a limited term of servitude was largely determined by the misfortunes incident to the voyage. This becomes apparent in the light of the multifarious causes which operated to empty the purse of the passengers, and leave them destitute on landing in America. Thousands who left their native country with sufficient means to pay their passages under favorable circumstances, and without ever dreaming of signing away their liberty by indenture, were, by adverse circumstances, compelled to submit to the conditions dictated by a master or a captain of a vessel in order to be landed. But the indenture and the burdens it imposed, were, to the majority, insignificant trials when compared to the hardships of the voyage itself.

During the early period of immigration, pirates and privateers swarmed the coast of America, and they did not hesitate to prey upon any commerce that was within their reach. At the beginning of the 18th century, it was estimated that no less than 15,000 engaged in this business, infested our coast. From Newfoundland to South America, ships were in danger of being captured as prizes and plundered at sea, or carried into Cape Fear or Providence.[1] The alarming extent to which this evil was carried, may be inferred from a letter of William Penn, in 1697, to Deputy Governor Mark-

---

[1] Pennsylvania German Society Publications; VIII: 84.

ham of Pennsylvania, charging the Provincial Council with having "not only countenanced, but actually encouraged pirates."[2] On his second return to Pennsylvania in 1699, Penn convened the Assembly for the purpose of enacting "two measures which in his opinion the existing state of affairs rendered imperative." One of these was "An act against pirates and privateers." In 1711 a scheme is laid before Governor Hunter of New York to guard the coasts against "the insults of French privateers which swarm the coasts where they not only take vast numbers of vessels, but have plundered several small towns and villages." This was an imminent danger which added to the dread of the long voyage. The German Pietists on their way to Pennsylvania in 1694, were attacked by three French privateers. A similar attempt was made on the vessel that brought Muhlenberg to Pennsylvania in 1742. His diary shows that all passengers were sometimes required to prepare for a defence: "Towards evening the captain ordered that every male person in the vessel should come on the quarterdeck and drill. They all came together, received their sabre, pistols, musket guns and powder. The captain showed each one the place where he should stand, in case a hostile attack should be made."[3]

The time of the voyage varied from five weeks to six months according to the conditions of the weather. William Penn's first voyage to America though under favorable circumstances, consumed two months; his return in 1684, seven weeks. Pastorius' voyage to Pennsylvania in the same year required ten weeks; another vessel leaving the same port and at the same time that Pastorius sailed, required three months to complete the journey. The second trip of William Penn in 1699 to America lasted more than three months. The Salzburgers sailed for the coast of Georgia in two transports, one leaving England the beginning of January, 1734, and reaching Charleston March 18th, the other leaving England October 28th, 1735, and reaching Charleston February 15th, 1736. Muhlenberg's voyage, in 1742, from the coast of England to Philadelphia, lasted over three months. The passengers of a vessel arriving in Philadelphia in 1748, were, on account of an accident and unfavorable winds kept on board six months and ten days.[4] The journey for those who came from southern Germany in 1754 lasted "fully half a year amid such hardships as no one is able to describe

---

[2] Penn. German Society, VIII: 82 ff.
[3] Penn. German Society, VIII: 92.
[4] H. E. Jacobs. Penn. Ger. Soc. VIII: 87.

adequately with their misery." [5] The passage from Holland to Cowes, England, alone, often required from two to four weeks.

The cost of transporting servants to Maryland in 1635 was estimated by Lord Baltimore, as being a little over 20 pounds per capita, including a year's provisions. [6] William Penn in 1682 estimated the cost of migration to Pennsylvania, "for man, woman, child and servant, as amounting to 20 pounds per capita." This estimate included "one year's keep until the land begins to produce crops." The actual cost was much higher than either of these estimates. [7] In 1708 Kocherthal, in a pamphlet on Carolina, [8] says, "In peace the fare is from five to six pounds sterling, but the cost of a convoy and other expenses raise it from seven to eight pounds for every adult." In 1720 the Palatines were sold for four and five years at ten pounds per head. Twenty years later, Peter Kalm says, "They commonly pay fourteen pounds Pennsylvania currency, for a person who is to serve four years and so on in proportion." [9]

During the middle of the 18th century, the cost from Rotterdam to Philadelphia, for all persons over ten years of age, was ten pounds; children from five to ten years of age, five pounds; children under five, free. "For these prices," says Mittleberger, [10] "the passengers are conveyed to Philadelphia, and as long as they are at sea, provided with food. But this is only the sea passage; the other costs on land, from home to Rotterdam, including the passage on the Rhine, are at least forty florins, no matter how economically one may live. No account is here taken of extraordinary contingencies. I may safely assert that with the greatest economy, many passengers have spent 200 florins (33 1-3 pounds) from home to Philadelphia." During the latter part of the 18th century, and the beginning of the 19th, redemptioners were sold for their passage, at from $40 to $100 for periods of two, three, and four years. On an average the passage at this time was about fifty dollars per capita. [11] In 1818 redemptioners were sold at Philadelphia at a somewhat higher rate. "The price for women," says Fearon, [12] "is about seventy dollars;

[5] Mittleberger's Journey to Pa. p. 18. Phila., 1898.

[6] A Relation of Maryland: 50; Ed. F. L. Hawks, Sabin's Reprints.

[7] Scharf and Wescott, Hist. of Phila: I: 142.

[8] Entitled, "Full and Circumstantial Report concerning the Renowned District of Carolina in English America." See Penn. Germ. Soc. VIII: 41.

[9] Peter Kalm, Travels, etc., II: 304.

[10] Journey to Pennsylvania: 26.

[11] Registry of Redemptioners, MSS.

[12] Sketches of America: 150.

men, eighty dollars; boys, sixty dollars." Of course the cost of servants who were sold for their passage, was in a large measure regulated by the demand and supply. Those who came as free willers or redemptioners, were often at the mercy of the captains, who sold them as high as possible to purchasers to whom they were bound by indenture.

Although occasionally a vessel is registered as sailing from Hamburg and Bremen, and late in the 18th century passengers arrived from Lisbon and the ports of France, the principal ports from which vessels of the continent sailed were Rotterdam and Amsterdam. The majority of the passengers who came from the Southern provinces of Germany, sailed in boats down the Rhine to Rotterdam, took passage to England and thence to America. To these the journey was extremely long and tedious. As late as 1750 the Rhine boats from Heilbronn to Holland passed thirty-six custom-houses, at all of which the ships were examined in detail, "when it suited the convenience of the custom-house officials." After arriving at Holland the passengers were detained five or six weeks. "Because things are dear there," writes a passenger in 1754, "the poor people have to spend nearly all they have during that time."[13] "Both in Rotterdam and Amsterdam the people are densely packed, in the large vessels. One person receives scarcely two feet width and six feet length in the bedstead, while many a ship carries four to six hundred souls; not to mention the innumerable implements, tools, provisions, waterbarrels and other things which likewise occupy much space."[14] After a journey which sometimes lasted four weeks the vessels arrived at some port in England, the most common one being Cowes. Here another delay of sometimes two weeks and even longer was encountered, during which custom duties were again collected and the vessels supplied with full cargoes for the ocean voyage. "During that time" says Mittleberger, "every one is compelled to spend his last remaining money and to consume his little stock of provisions which had been reserved for the sea; so that most passengers, finding themselves on the ocean where they would be in greater need of them, must greatly suffer from hunger and want."[15] But the greatest suffering to the majority of those who came from the continent via England was while crossing the ocean. The shipping regulations in Holland before

[13] Mittleberger's Journey to Pa.: p. 18.
[14] Ibid.
[15] Ibid: 19.

1755 were very remiss concerning passengers. No attempt seems to have been made to prevent frauds or to protect the rights of immigrants. Confusion and disorder prevailed on embarking. Sometimes one vessel was loaded almost entirely with baggage and chests which the passengers had filled with provisions for the voyage, and upon which the poor people unable to secure the necessities of life, largely depended. Other vessels were loaded almost entirely with passengers without regard to the necessary amount of provisions. "Many who at home had owned property, and converted it into money were robbed *intransitu*, by the ship owners, importers, sea captains and Neulanders. The emigrants' chests with their clothes, and sometimes their money were put on other vessels or ships, and left behind," [16]

A letter of Christopher Sauer, dated March 15, 1755, shows the lawless manner in which the shipping was carried on at Holland. It appears that at times monopolies were granted to certain individuals who controlled the shipping. The profit in passengers being much greater than in merchandise, vessels were sometimes so crowded with the latter that many were kept upon the upper deck, exposed to all kinds of weather. As a result the majority of these died, "so that in less than one year two thousand were buried in the sea." But the death of a passenger after more than one-half the voyage had been made, did not lessen the profit to the merchants, since relatives and friends of the deceased were held responsible for the payment of their passage. Under these unfavorable conditions it is not strange that the majority who landed at Philadelphia should be sold as servants. Contracts made with the avaricious merchants in Holland were disregarded. "When the ignorant Germans" says a writer, "agree fairly with the merchants at Holland for seven pistoles and a half, when they come to Philadelphia the merchants make them pay whatever they please, and take at least nine pistoles, the poor people on board being prisoners and at the mercy of the captains. Anxious to come ashore to satisfy hunger, they pay whatever is demanded * * * * and when their chests are put into stores, and by the time they have procured money of their friends to pay for what they have agreed, and more too, and demand their chests, they find them opened and plundered of their contents; or sometimes they are not to be found." [17] Instances have occurred

---

[16] Benjamin Rush, Manners of the Early Germans of Pennsylvania; pp. 6, 7.

[17] Quoted in Rupp, Hist. of Northumberland, etc.: 55-57. Lancaster, 1847.

4

where the Holland merchants made a secret contract with the captains to send passengers bound for Pennsylvania to another port in America, where the price of servants was higher. "Thus emigrants are compelled in Holland to submit to the wind and the captain's will."[18]   In addition to the trials incident to an over-crowded vessel, were added those of an insufficient and inferior supply of food. Those who were not supplied with an extra stock of provisions, or whose chests containing the same, had been shipped in another vessel or left behind, in nearly all cases suffered for want of food; and in case the voyage was extended beyond the ordinary time by adverse winds, or from other causes, starvation was the result. In fact a long voyage under the greatest precaution, rendered it difficult to carry sufficient provisions and keep them in good condition during the entire voyage.[19]

Under such conditions the rate of mortality was necessarily large. Scot, who chartered a ship to transport 130 passengers to East Jersey in 1685, lost thirty-five during the voyage, by deaths, and there is no account of any unusual accident to the vessel or to the passengers.[20] In 1732 a ship that had been at sea four months, lost 100 out of 150 passengers by starvation. Another vessel, seventeen weeks in its journey, lost sixty of its passengers. A ship sailing from Rotterdam in 1738 with four hundred Palatines lost seventy-seven per cent. of its passengers whose deaths were assigned to the bad condition of the water taken at Rotterdam. A vessel arriving at Philadelphia in 1745 landed but fifty survivors out of four hundred, most of the deaths having resulted from starvation.

---

[18] Mittleberger, Journey to Pa.: 40.

[19] Daniel Pastorius, in a letter of March 7, 1684, says "The fare on board was very bad. Every ten persons received each week three pounds of butter; daily four cans of beer, and two cans of water; at noon every day in the week, meat and fish three days, at noon, which we had to dress, with our own butter; and every day we had to keep enough from our dinner to make our supper upon."—Pennypacker's Settlement of Germantown: 82.
Mittleberger, in 1750, says, "Warm food is served only three times a week, the ration being very poor and very little * * * * The water which is served out on the ships is often very black, thick, and full of worms, so that one cannot drink it without loathing, even with the greatest thirst. Toward the end we were compelled to eat the ship's biscuits which had been spoiled long ago; though in a whole biscuit there was scarcely a piece the size of a dollar that had not been full of red worms and spiders' nests. Great hunger and thirst forced us to eat everything."—Journey to Pennsylvania: 24.

[20] W. A. Whitehead, Contributions, etc., p. 27.

A report on the condition of redemptioners on board an American
vessel sailing to New York in 1805, and addressed to H. Muhlenberg, president of the German Society of Philadelphia, reveals a
wretched condition to which passengers were compelled to submit
at the hands of a heartless captain. This vessel loaded with German passengers, leaving the port of Tönnigen, arrived after fourteen days at an English port. During her four weeks stay here an
English recruiting officer came on board and the passengers were
given an opportunity to enlist in the British service. Ten
men consented to enlist, giving as their reason for so doing,
that "they were apprehensive that should they stay on board the
ship they should be starved before they arrived in America." It
will be remembered that it was during this period that the question
of enlistment was one of the great controversies between England
and America, and one of the alleged causes of the war of 1812.
The treatment these passengers received after leaving England is
related as follows: "After fourteen days had elapsed the captain
informed them that they would get nothing to eat except bread and
meat. After this each person received two biscuits, one pint of
water and the eighth part of a pound of meat per day. This regulation continued for two or three weeks. * * * * The hunger
and thirst being at this time so great, and the children continually
crying for bread and drink, some of the men, resolved, at all
events, to procure bread, broke open the apartment wherein it was
kept, and took some. The whole of the passengers were punished
for this offense. The men received no bread, and the women but
one biscuit. This continued for nine days, when the men were
again allowed one biscuit per day. In this situation their condition
became dreadful, so much so that five and twenty men, women and
children actually perished for want of the common necessaries of
life, in short for want of bread. The hunger was so great on board
that all the bones about the ship were hunted up by them, pounded
with a hammer and eaten; and what is more lamentable, some of
the deceased persons, not many hours before their death, crawled
on their hands and feet to the captain, and begged him, for God's
sake, to give them a mouthful of bread or a drop of water to keep
them from perishing, but their supplications were in vain; he most
obstinately refused, and thus did they perish." [21]

[21] Copied from the records of the German Society of Philadelphia. See
F. Kapp, Immigration and the Commissioners of Emigration of the State of
New York; appendix: 138.

With no attention paid to sanitation, fevers and other contagious diseases were common scourges which added greatly to the rate of mortality.[22] Mittleberger, writing of the conditions as they existed in the middle of the 18th century, says, "Children from one to seven years rarely survive the voyage.[23] Hunger, thirst, affliction, home-sickness, anxiety and neglect, added to the cruel treatment often received at the hands of the sailors, frequently caused the passengers to rise in mutiny against the officers of the vessel, and quarrels and riots arose among friends.[24]

Before 1708, the vessels were less crowded than during the later periods of immigration. Before the great German influx, the majority of passengers came from Great Britain, and in that country the shipping regulations, though often avoided, were much better than in Holland. But even during the first period, from 1682 to 1708, there was scarcely a vessel arrived at Pennsylvania, in which there were no deaths during the voyage. The voyage of William Penn who exercised the strictest discipline and caution, resulted in some deaths. Of the four hundred Palatines who sailed for New York in 1709, twenty per cent. died on the voyage.[25] The number of deaths in fifteen vessels, in 1738, are estimated at from 1600 to 2000.[26] As late as 1818, Fearon, an English traveler in America, visiting a ship lying in the harbor at Philadelphia, observes, "that they crammed into one of those vessels, 500 passengers, eighty of whom died on the passage." [27] In vessels where sickness prevailed, mortality by no means ceased on landing, or on the vessel's arrival. While lying in the harbor awaiting the details and delays of the

---

[22] Pennsylvania German Society Publications; VIII: 93-96.

[23] "Many a time parents are compelled to see their children miserably suffer and die from hunger, thirst and sickness, and then see them cast into the water. I witnessed such a misery in no less than thirty-two children in our ship all of whom were thrown into the sea. * * * * Children who have not yet had the measles or smallpox generally get them on board the ship, and mostly die of them * * * * sometimes whole families die in quick succession; so that often many dead persons lie in the berths beside the living ones, especially when contagious diseases have broken out on board the ship."—Journey to Pennsylvania: 23.

[24] "Children cry out against their parents, husbands against their wives, and wives against their husbands; brothers and sisters, friends and acquaintances, against each other."—Ibid: 22.

[25] S. H. Cobb, The Palatine Immigration to New York and Pennsylvania: 22.

[26] Pennsylvania German Society; VIII: 94.

[27] Sketches of America: 150.

custom house officials, a large number perished before medical assistance could prevent the havoc of disease; in fact such assistance was of little avail while the patients were confined to their filthy lodgings. In the summer of 1754, 253 were buried in Philadelphia, after having arrived at the port.

As a result of these conditions, Philadelphia was exposed to constant danger from malignant and contagious fevers brought there by passengers from the vessels, the causes of which are given in a report by the Health officers to the Governor and Council in 1754: "The steam of bilge water and the breath of great Numbers of people betwixt the decks of a ship make the air moist and in some degree putrid, and like that of Marshy and Boggy places will produce fevers on persons that are a long time in them, but these fevers are not contagious and require no other precaution but separating the sick and keeping them in places well air'd and cleaned. * * * * But when to the state of the air any considerable degree of animal putrifaction is added either from uncleanness, or too great a confinement of the air itself, then it produces a fever, malignant in its nature, and contagious." [28]

After arriving at Philadelphia passengers who were unable to pay for their passage were kept on board until sold. The manner in which passengers were disposed of on landing is so vividly told by Mittleberger who arrived in 1750, and whose description seems to correspond with the facts, that a somewhat extended extract is here given: "When after a long and tedious voyage, the ship comes in sight of land, so that the promontories can be seen, which the people were so eager and anxious to see, all creep from below on deck to see the land from afar, and they weep with joy, and pray

---

[28] The following account was given to the Governor by the Health Officers: "Captain Arthur told us that in the year 1741 they took in a parcel of convicts from the Dublin Goal and other servants from the City; soon after the people on board were seized with fevers, which few escaped, so that they were in great distress from the number of sick during the whole voyage. Where these people were landed we did not inquire; but this ship after they were out was brought to Hamilton's Wharf and from thence carried to Thomas Penrose's to be repaired. Soon after her coming to the Wharf seven persons in the family of Anthony Morris the elder, and several in the house of Anthony Morris the younger, were seized with putrid bilious Fevers, and seventeen of Mr. Penrose's family who had been on board the ship were likewise affected with the same fever, and also sundry other persons in every part of that neighborhood where the Ballast of the Ship was thrown. This Fever afterwards raged through the City to the loss of many of its valuable inhabitants."—Penna. German Soc. VIII: 94.

and sing, thanking and praising God. The sight of the land makes
the people on board the ship, especially the sick and the half dead,
alive again, so that their hearts leap within them; they shout and
rejoice, and are content to bear their misery in patience, in the hope
that they may soon reach the land in safety. But alas! When the
ships have landed at Philadelphia after their long voyage, no one
is permitted to leave them except those who pay for their passage
or can give good security; the others who cannot pay, must remain
on board the ships till they are all purchased, and are released from
the ships by the purchasers. The sick always fare the worst, for
the healthy are naturally preferred and purchased first; and so the
sick and wretched must often remain on board in front of the city
for two or three weeks, and frequently die, whereas many a one if
he could pay his debts and were permitted to leave the ship immediately, might recover and remain alive." The sale of passengers
on board the ship is thus described: "Every day Englishmen,
Dutchmen and High-German people come from the City of Philadelphia and other places, in part from a great distance, say 20, 30, or
40 miles away, and go on board the newly arrived ship that has
brought and offers for sale passengers from Europe, and select
among the healthy persons such as they deem suitable for their
business, and bargain with them how long they will serve for their
passage money, which most of them are still in debt for. When
they have come to an agreement it happens that adult persons bind
themselves in writing to serve 3, 4, 5 or 6 years for the amount due
by them according to their strength. But very young people, from
10 to 15 years, must serve till they are 21 years old. Parents must
sell and trade away their children like so many cattle; for if the
children can take the debt upon themselves, the parents can leave
the ship free and unrestrained; but as the parents often do not
know where or to what people their children are going, it often happens that such parents and children, after leaving the ship, do not
see each other again for many years, perhaps no more in all their
lives." [29]

The above description is not overdrawn, though it represents
the system in the time of its greatest abuse. The condition of passengers before they were sold, and in fact the sale itself, differed
little from that of actual slaves. In the following description which
is given by an eye witness to the sales on board the vessel, all but
the auction block is represented: "Die Zeitungen machen bekanut,

[29] Mittleberger, Journey to Pa. pp. 25, 26, 27.

so und so viel Deutsche sein für ihre Fracht und Schulden zu verkaufen. Nun geht der markt auf dem Schiffe los. Wer einen
Knecht, eine Magd braucht, geht hin und sucht sich das Passende
aus. Die Schiffs meister suchen die Lente hoch auszubringen und
als gesund und kräftig darzustellen, die Kaufer aber wollen sie nied-
rig erhandlen und betasten und beurtheilen sie wie Sklaven."[30]
Before the formation of the German Society, in 1764, passengers infected with disease were as a rule not permitted to land until a certificate from the Health officer, testifying to their fitness was obtained, or until it was evident that no purchaser could be secured.[31]

Upon the arrival of a vessel, all passengers in sound condition
were "arranged in long columns, led to a magistrate, compelled to
take the oath of allegiance to the English King, then marched back
to the dreaded ship to be sold."[32] Children above ten years of age,
could assume the debt of the parents, thus releasing the latter from
indenture by extending their own time of service. "When people
arrive who cannot make themselves free, but have children under
5 years, the parents cannot free themselves by them; for such children must be given to somebody without compensation to be
brought up till they are 21 years old."[33] Those from five to ten
years of age were compelled to serve until the age of twenty-one.
The wife was compelled to serve for the husband in case of the
latter's inability; and in like manner the husband was responsible
for the debt of his wife whose term of indenture was added to his,
thus extending the time of service to five or six years. "But if both
are sick they are sent to the Hospital, but not until it appears prob-
able that they will find no purchasers. After recovering they are
compelled to serve as the rest."[34] The surviving relatives of those
who died at sea after the vessel had made more than one-half the

[30] Hallischen Nachrichten, Quoted in Loehr's Geschichte und Zustande,
etc.; p. 79, et seq.

[31] Health Office Oct. 5, 1815, Sir:—I do hereby certify that Captain Benjamin K. Harrison of Ship Baloon has entered Twenty-five passengers from
Amsterdam, the whole of them in perfect hearty condition.

                                        JAMES PH. PUGLIA,
                                                Health Officer.

AND'W LEINEAN, ESQ.
        Register of German Passengers.
Copied from MSS. in Hist. Soc. of Penn.

[32] See Appendix. IV.
[33] Mittleberger, Journey to Pa. 27.
[34] Ibid: 28.

journey, were held responsible for the debts of the deceased. In these disposals, husband, wife, and children were often sold to different purchasers, until a law was passed prohibiting the separation of husband and wife without their consent.

The general demand for servants in the colony gave rise to a class of dealers, called "soul-drivers," who found it profitable to retail servants among the farmers. They purchased the servants of the Captains in lots of fifty or more, and drove them through the country like so many cattle to dispose of them at whatever price they could. Sometimes they would go to Europe, collect a lot, and bring them to this country, to avoid the intervention of the merchants. In this case the indenture was made out before leaving Europe, and the soul-driver made an arrangement with the captain for transporting the entire lot. In about 1785 the soul-drivers disappear. Public sentiment was becoming strongly opposed to this manner of disposal, and as a result the number that ran away from the dealers became too large to enable them to carry on their traffic with profit.[35] The financial arrangements under which passengers were transported varied according to the transporters, and the financial condition of the passengers. The vast majority of those from Germany, after 1727, being without means, depended, as has been seen, upon their entire passage being paid by their purchasers and masters on landing. Some merchants, however, made private contracts with passengers, requiring them to pay one-half of the passage fees upon embarking, and the other half six weeks after landing. But when no purchaser could be found, they were sold by the owner or master of the vessel arbitrarily, and were compelled to submit entirely to whatever terms he chose to make.[36] Under

---

[35] History of Delaware County (Pa.) p. 348. Phila., 1862.

One of these soul-drivers who transacted business in Chester, was tricked by one of his redemptioners in the following manner: "The fellow by a little management, contrived to be the last of the flock that remained unsold, and traveled about with his owner without companions. One night they lodged at a tavern, and in the morning, the young fellow who was an Irishman, rose early and sold his master to the landlord, pocketed the money, and marched off. Previously, however, to his going, he used the precaution to tell the purchaser, that his servant, although tolerably clever in other respects, was rather saucy and a little given to lying,—that he had even presumption enough at times to endeavor to pass for master, and that he might possibly represent himself so to him. By the time mine host was undeceived, the son of Erin had gained such a start as rendered pursuit hopeless."—History of Delaware County: 348.

[36] Georgia Historical Society Collection, II: 78. Savannah, 1842.

whatever conditions the passengers came, if they were unable to pay all the expenses incurred by them during the voyage, an indenture was required to insure the liquidation of the debt. Under such conditions the servant was unable to choose his master; his wishes in this regard were not consulted, and consequently, his fortunate or unfortunate relation during his period of service was a matter of accident.[37]

Many Germans who had enough money to pay their passage, preferred being sold as servants with a view that during their service they might learn the language and the conditions of the country, and thus be better able to determine what to do after they had obtained their freedom.[38] The contract drawn up in Holland, between the passengers and merchants was in English, and as the Germans were ignorant of the language, it was an easy matter for the captains and merchants to disregard it on landing, while the reluctance to litigate, common to the Germans, as in fact, it is to any foreigners unacquainted with the laws of the country, was sufficiently great to prevent them from enforcing their rights by presenting their wrongs to a magistrate. Unless friends came to their rescue they were entirely at the mercy of the ship owners and transporters, and were compelled to submit to whatever terms might be offered, which they often accepted at a dear price in order to escape the misery of the ship.

The condition of the English and Irish servants on the journey, was much the same as that of the Germans. When after 1730, the Irish begin to arrive in large numbers, their complaints are frequent, and petitions against abuses of transportation are made in behalf of Irish as well as German. But it was the preponderance of German immigration over that of other nations into Pennsylvania that made the abuses of transportation from the continent especially prominent. The English speaking immigrants, to be sure, possessed certain natural advantages over the Germans. A knowledge of the language, laws, and customs prevented in a

---

[37] Not infrequently romantic incidents, illustrated in such works of fiction as "Moll Flanders," "Colonel Jack," and "Janice Meredith," attached themselves to these sales. Fearon relates the following which is also mentioned by Samuel Breck in his "Recollections:" "A gentleman of this city (Philadelphia) wanted an old couple to take care of his house;—a man, his wife, and daughter were offered to him for sale;—he purchased them. They proved to be his father, his mother, and sister!!!"—Sketches of America: 151.

[38] Peter Kalm, Travels, II: 304. London, 1772.

measure the disregard of agreements by the merchants so frequently practiced on the Germans. George Alsop, who served four years in Maryland, represents the condition of English servants on the voyage and in the colonies very favorably, in a pamphlet [*] published in 1665. He says that the passengers on the voyage have sufficient provisions, that "they want for nothing that is necessary and convenient," he denies the frequent charges made that they "are sold in open markets for slaves." Though the conditions of servants at the early period to which he refers were much more favorable than during the middle of the 18th century, his statements must be taken with reserve, and are to be regarded as the exception rather than the rule. Being himself a servant, his account which is much quoted is naturally regarded as one of the few trustworthy descriptions which give an insight into the system of indentured service during the middle of the 17th century. With respect to the condition and treatment of servants, however, its trustworthiness is greatly impaired by the apparent fact, that it was written in the interest of Merchant adventurers in order to encourage emigration, and to counteract the influence of the numerous unfavorable reports of the system circulated throughout England.

A century later, William Eddis, an English traveler in America, represents the condition of English servants to be entirely different from that described by Alsop. He regards the system as differing little from slavery. The manner in which redemptioners or free willers are disposed of on landing is described as follows: "It is an article of agreement with these deluded victims, that if they are not successful in obtaining situations, on their own terms, within a certain number of days after their arrival in the country, they are to be sold in order to defray the charges of the passage, at the discretion of the master of the vessel, or the agent to whom he is consigned in the Province. * * * * Servants are rarely permitted to set foot on shore until they have absolutely formed their respective engagements. As soon as the ship is stationed in her berth, planters, mechanics, and others, repair on board; the adventurers of both sexes are exposed to view and very few are happy enough to make their own stipulations, * * * * and even when this is obtained the advantages are by no means equivalent to their sanguine expectations. The residue stung with disappointment and vexation meet with horror the moment which dooms

---

[*] George Alsop, "A Character of the Province of Maryland" published in Md. Hist. Soc. Fund Publications, No. 13-18. Baltimore, 1878.

them, under an appearance of equity to a limited term of slavery." [40] A still worse condition is represented by one who visited a ship nearly fifty years later, loaded with redemptioners. It was a vessel that arrived in the harbor of Philadelphia in 1817: "As we ascended the side of the hulk, a most revolting scene of want and misery presented itself. The eye involuntarily turned for some relief from the horrible picture of human suffering which this living sepulchre afforded. Mr. ——— enquired if there were any shoemakers on board. The captain advanced: his appearance bespoke his office; he was an American, tall, determined, and with an eye that flashed with Algerine cruelty. He called in the Dutch language for shoemakers, and never can I forget the scene which followed. The poor fellows came running up with unspeakable delight, no doubt anticipating a relief from their loathsome dungeon. Their clothes, if rags deserve that denomination, actually perfumed the air. Some were without shirts, others had this article of dress, but of a quality as coarse as the worst packing cloth. * * * * When they saw at our departure that we had not purchased, their countenances fell to that standard of stupid gloom which seemed to place them a link below rational beings." [41]

There was this general and important difference between the immigrants from the continent and those from Great Britain: The majority of the former came as redemptioners or free willers, that is to say, the indenture was issued upon landing in America. Under these conditions an agreement between the passengers and the merchants or masters of vessels in Holland, was all that was required. Consequently there was no occasion for the authorities in those ports to take measures other than those required for ordinary immigrants who paid their passage. No checks or limitations could well be put upon a system that had no legal basis. Hope lured the immigrant on to the colony, and it was not until he landed that he became fully

---

[40] William Eddis, Letters from America: 74-75. London, 1792.

[41] Fearon, Sketches of America: 149-50. It is interesting to note that the vessel which Fearon represents as being American with an "American" captain, is claimed by Walsh to have been a British vessel. "She was British property and navigated on British account; her crew was British, and her captain an Englishman, by the name of William Garterell. On arriving at Philadelphia he selected as his factors, the Messrs. Odlin & Co., merchants of that city, whom Fearon falsely represents as the owners of the vessel." Whatever merit there may be in the criticism, there seems to be no doubt about the truthfulness of the condition of the passengers as described by Fearon. See Walsh, An Appeal, etc., preface: xxviii.

cognizant of the conditions into which he entered. It was only by means of courts or a system of registration that the authorities of Holland could determine the status of those who left their ports; and, as a monopoly of the shipping was often granted to merchants, it is not strange that the abuses reached such enormous proportions. The majority of the English and the Irish, on the other hand, came as indentured servants, that is, the indenture was signed, and the relation of master and servant established before embarking. Under these arrangements the condition and plan of the system was constantly brought to the notice of the English authorities; it was put on a legal basis in England. Courts of registration were established and no servants, except convicts, could legally be transported against their will though in practice the laws were often evaded.

CHAPTER VI.

LAWS AND METHODS OF REGULATING TRANSPORTA-
TION.

The evils arising from the methods of transporting servants and other passengers, were the natural results of a system which gave profitable employment to so many different classes. The merchants, the masters of vessels, the Neulanders, the "spirits" and the "soul-drivers,"—all found it profitable to bring as many passengers as possible in a single vessel to the colonies. It is not at all strange that ships were crowded far beyond their capacity, which resulted at times in an enormous death rate. Against these evils frequent petitions were sent by the colonial assemblies to the home government in England, and urgent letters from influential citizens of Pennsylvania to the authorities in Holland. From England, where the system of indenture had been fully developed long before the colony of Pennsylvania was founded, came the first act of relief. A petition from the merchants in America, asking for some regular method of transporting servants to the plantations, was considered by the Council Board in 1664, and by the Council of Plantations in 1670, and resulted in the adoption of a definite plan of transportation in 1682. Every servant was required to sign the indenture in the presence of a magistrate or other officer authorized or appointed for the purpose. A Clerk of the Peace was to keep a record of the names of the persons bound; of the Magistrate before whom the indenture was executed, and of the time and place of said execution. No person above twenty-one years of age was to be bound unless the magistrate before whom he appeared was "wholly satisfied from him of his free and voluntary agreement to enter into the said service." No person between the ages of fourteen and twenty-one, could be bound without the consent of parent or master, and "some person that knows the said servant to be of the name mentioned in the indenture." Those under fourteen years of age were required to have the consent of the parents, or "not to be carried on ship-board till a fortnight at least after he becomes bound, to the intent that if there be any abuse it may be discovered before he be trans-ported. And when his parents do not appear before the magistrates,

notice is to be sent to them, or, where they cannot be found, to the
church wardens or overseers of the Parish where he was last settled,
in such manner as the magistrates shall think fit and direct." [1]

The encouragement given by the Board of Trade to the importation of servants during the early years of the province of Pennsylvania did much to bring on the abuses which later demanded such
stringent regulations. In 1684 an "Act to encourage the importation of Servants" was read and approved by that body.[2] England
was especially desirous of providing a place for a large class of her
population under twenty-one years of age, "lurking about in divers
parts of London and elsewhere, who want employment, and may
be tempted to become thieves if not provided for." It was this class
which gave merchants the greatest trouble, and especially brought
the system of transportation into disrepute. If, after arriving in
America, their wildest hopes were not realized, they would complain
that they had been treacherously persuaded to take passage to
America; and, as many unsuspecting persons were actually deceived
or forced on board by the secret agents of merchants, much credence
was given to the complaints of this idle and shiftless class. It was
under the act of 1682, providing that no one under twenty-one years
of age could be bound without the consent of parents or masters,
that this class found ground for complaint, as they were without
masters and disclaimed by their parents. Legally they could not
be transported. An act accordingly was passed in the fourth year
of George I, providing that 'where any person fifteen to twenty-one
years of age shall be willing to be transported and to enter into any
service in any of his Majesties' Colonies or plantations in America,
it shall be lawful for any merchant to contract with any such person
for any service not exceeding the term of eight years,' providing,
however, that the indenture be acknowledged before the Mayor of
London or some Justice of the Peace."

The large number of "unhealthy vessels" landing passengers in
the province was early brought to the notice of the colonial authorities, and was the occasion of many discussions between the
Governor and Assembly. An act in 1700 provided that "no
unhealthy or sickly vessels coming from any sickly place whatsoever shall come nearer than one mile to any of the towns or ports

---

[1] Board of Trade Journals—Transcripts. 1675—1782. IV: 79. Historical Society of Penn.

[2] Board of Trade Journals, Vol. V. 1684-86, Transcripts in Historical
Society of Pennsylvania.

in this Province." [*] No passengers or goods could be landed, until a license from the Governor and Council, or from two Justices of the Peace, was granted testifying to their healthy condition. This act was by later legislation frequently modified and finally repealed in 1774. No provision had as yet been made for the landing or disposing of sick passengers. As the ships at this period were not yet so crowded as they later were,—an evil so difficult to remedy,—there was at this time no demand for any action along this line. Those who were sick during the voyage were then a small proportion of the passengers, and were usually able to land after lying in the harbor a few weeks. But with the increase of immigration came an increase of sickness and deaths. The vessels became too crowded to accommodate even the sick, and many deaths resulted from the neglect of passengers while lying in the harbor. As the citizens were naturally reluctant to receive even their own relatives infected with disease, the question occasioned much alarm and discussion. Repeatedly the inhabitants of the Province petitioned the Governor to provide some suitable place for receiving the sick, but as the Assembly considered it a part of their patriotic duty to oppose nearly every measure recommended by the Governor, it was not until 1742 that the requests were acted upon. The tardiness which characterized the Assembly in remedial legislation along this line, was partly due to the fact that the majority of the passengers were Germans whose political influence was constantly increasing, and who were naturally regarded with more or less jealous apprehensions by the English Colonists.

In 1741 several of the most influential Germans sent a petition to Governor Thomas setting forth that for want of a convenient house for the reception of their countrymen who had contracted disease during the long voyage, they were obliged to continue on board of the ships which brought them where they could get neither attendance nor conveniences suitable to their condition; that as a result of these conditions many had lost their lives. To remedy these evils they asked the Governor to recommend to the Assembly the erection, at the public expense, of a suitable building for the reception of the sick. Governor Thomas presented the matter to the Assembly with his recommendation, and after considerable discussion an act was passed, in 1742, providing for the purchase of a site called, Province Island. The purchase consisted of 342 acres,

---

[*] A Collection of the Laws of the Province of Pennsylvania, Now in force. p. 25. Phila., 1742.

six of which were set apart for the erection of a Pest-house, and to this "all sick and infectious persons" were sent. Their nursing was to be paid by the master or owner of the vessel who in turn was paid from the effects of the passengers.[4]

As the number of immigrants increased, new abuses required new regulations. The early provincial laws attempted to correct abuses of transportation by negative legislation only; evils were prohibited without substituting positive legal remedies. Such laws were consequently inadequate, and it was usually not long after they were passed that merchants found a channel of evasion by which they carried on the traffic in a manner not less destructive of the welfare of the province. An illustration of these conditions is afforded in a law passed in 1700 which prohibited the landing of passengers infected with contagious disease; but since no positive provision was made for their disposal or care, they were landed secretly, and thus defeated the purpose of the law, until hospital regulations were provided in 1749. Laws were passed during the early period of the province against importing convicts and lunatics in order to protect the country from an improvident and shiftless class; but these were likewise evaded by those engaged in the passenger traffic. When, upon the arrival of a vessel in the harbor, the custom house officials had designated what passengers might legally be landed, no offer or attempt at landing the unwelcome convict was made; but no sooner had the provincial officers apparently completed their work, than the captain began to wait for opportunities by many and various ways to smuggle the forbidden passengers ashore. To provide against this illicit traffic, a law was passed in 1729 requiring all masters of vessels, merchants, and others, who imported passengers and servants, to make an entry before the Collector of Customs of the names of all passengers on board, and this within twenty-four hours after the vessel had arrived. It was required that the mayor of Philadelphia or any two Justices of the town or county where the passengers were to be landed, be notified of the arrival of every vessel. Importers were called before these officials and examined upon oath concerning the number and condition of those designed to be landed. Certificates were then issued to the officials of the vessel containing the names of those passengers who were deemed worthy of becoming citizens, and only such were permitted to land

---

[4] Acts of the Assembly of the Province of Pennsylvania: 194, 196, 197. Phila., 1775.

under the direction of officers appointed for the purpose.[5] The same act placed a duty of five pounds on every convict imported. The real purpose of this was to exclude the importation of this class altogether; in addition to the heavy duty, one-half of which was to go to the informer or the collector, the masters importing them were required to give security to the amount of fifty pounds for their good behavior. This, no master could afford to do. As England had encouraged and expressly enjoined the importation of convicts and vagabonds, this law of the Assembly was practically in conflict with the English statutes on this subject.

Though an act was passed in 1742 providing for the erection of a hospital, from a petition five years later, it appears that no suitable arrangements had been made for the care of the sick who continued to increase with the increase of immigration; for in the spring of 1749 a petition from the inhabitants of Philadelphia was presented to the House setting forth the practice of the merchants concerned in the importation of Germans and other foreigners into the province; they complained that vessels were crowded beyond their capacity; that disease had been produced among the passengers, which resulted in the loss of hundreds in a single vessel; that the surviving relatives had been obliged by their own labor to defray the passage money of the dead; that besides the injury done to the Germans by this iniquitous and infamous practice, the inhabitants had become greatly endangered by the importation of mortal distempers; that for want of suitable buildings and other conveniences, the sick had been induced to wander from one place to another, without care, and to the manifest danger of the inhabitants. They asked that the House make provision for the prevention of such practices, for the relief of those strangers, and for the safety of the inhabitants.[6]

This petition resulted in a more complete regulation of the passenger traffic. "An Act for Prohibiting the Importation of too Many Germans in one vessel" was immediately passed. It provided that no Master of any ship bound to Philadelphia or elsewhere in the Province should import any greater number of passengers in any one vessel than could be suitably provided for; every passenger of the age of fourteen years or upwards was to have a berth at least six feet in length, and one foot six inches in breadth; and if under

---

[5] Charters and Acts of Assembly of the Province of Pa.: 122. Phila., 1762.

[6] Colonial Records, V: 427.

5

fourteen years of age, to contain the same length and breadth for every two such passengers. For every violation of this act, the Master or Commander, was to pay a penalty of ten pounds. The officers appointed for collecting duties, were required in going on board newly arrived vessels to inform themselves of the condition of passengers, and to report any neglect to the Mayor or Alderman of Philadelphia. It seems to have been the custom, or at least a frequent practice, of the masters of vessels to confiscate the property of the deceased in payment of their passage after the ships had arrived in the harbor. To prevent this an inventory of the deceased was demanded from every master or captain, which was to be presented to the Register-General or to some of his deputies of the county in which the vessel arrived; after the payment of all dues to the master of the vessel, the property was restored to the relatives or creditors of the deceased. Neglect to furnish a true inventory was punishable by a fine of 100 pounds.[1]

But however rigorous the attempts to remedy the evils, legislation up to 1765 was by no means adequate to control the passenger traffic, or to correct the abuses which necessarily caused many to be unjustly bound to service. It was not long after an act had been passed, that masters of vessels found a way of violating the spirit if not the letter of the law. In the act of 1749, for example, which was primarily intended to prevent the importation of passengers in too great numbers in a single vessel by specifying the space that each passenger should have, no provision was made for the height of each berth. Vessels were still crowded as much as before that act was passed. To comply with the two dimensions specified by law, the berths were so constructed as to reduce the former height, thus giving no increase in the number of cubic feet per capita. On the whole the conditions through the middle of the century were bad. The increase of immigration brought with it an increase of disorder. The sick were neglected; contracts made in Europe between importers and passengers were disregarded; immigrants were sold into service to pay the fare of friends or relatives who had died on the journey; husband, wife and children were still separated by being sold to different masters; passengers were robbed of their baggage on landing, and held and treated as prisoners until sold.

These abuses brought into existence an organization which exerted a potent influence in ameliorating the condition of the immigrant. In 1764 a number of influential Germans of Philadelphia

---

[1] Acts of the Assembly of the Province of Pa., pp. 223, 224. Phila., 1775.

organized the "German Society of Pennsylvania." Its object was to assist their countrymen in establishing themselves in the colony, and especially to correct the abuses of transportation. A constitution was drafted providing for regular meetings and a systematic mode of action. In their first meeting it was voted to send an English copy of their constitution to the Governor, asking his support in their efforts. An address was also sent to the Assembly requesting better laws regarding the transportation of Germans. Their address to the Governor states that the Germans gratefully recognize the hospitality shown them by the English; that duty directed them to mitigate the sufferings of their countrymen; that the Germans were strong enough in the Province to take care of themselves, and only asked a helping hand in cases where cruel injustice to immigrants could thus be avoided. Their petition to the Assembly contained a project for protecting and regulating the passenger traffic. This was January 1, 1765. Ten days later the matter was considered by the Assembly and a bill was passed embodying the requests of the Society and presented to the Governor for his signature. However, as the matter was presented to the Governor at the end of the session he deferred signing it and requested it to be put over to the next session for further deliberation.

The project presented to the Assembly by the German Society is not only important as showing the work of this organization and its relation to legislation in behalf of German immigrants, but it also gives an idea of the abuses still existing in regard to immigration in 1765. In this petition they ask: that the custom officers appointed by the government should be accompanied by a German interpreter who should go on board every vessel and explain to the German passengers such portions of the acts of the Assembly as pertain to the landing of passengers; that masters of vessels give a receipt to each passenger for his baggage on embarking; that the contract made between masters of vessels and immigrants in Europe be strictly carried out; that passengers who had paid their full fare immediately receive their goods on landing; that no one be bound for the freight of relatives who died on the voyage; that no one be bound for another, except a man for his wife and children; that passengers owing for their freight should not be treated and held as prisoners for an indefinite length of time; that the sick be better cared for; that no warrants of arrest be issued for the payment of freight, unless one-half be not paid within twelve months after landing, or in case the debtor attempted to leave the province; that all contracts made between captain and passenger on the voyage for the payment of freight be null and void; that the indenture only apply to the province of Pennsylvania; that no one be sold out of the province; and finally, that man and wife be not separated by the sale.

The German Society exerted a considerable influence on legislation in later years. They recommended to the Assembly many officers who were in a large measure to control the affairs of German immigrants. The petition sent to the Assembly by this Society, January 1st, and considered by them on the 11th, was again brought up in that body May 18th, was signed by the Governor and became a law. It provided among other things that the room allotted to each passenger by the previous act should also be at least 3 feet 9 inches in height, in the fore part of the ship, between decks, and at least two feet nine inches in the cabin and steerage. It further provided that each vessel should have an able surgeon for the use of passengers at the charge of the owner; that twice every week during the voyage the vessel should be thoroughly cleansed and disinfected. Provisions were to be sold at a profit not exceeding 50 per cent. on the first cost. Officers on visiting the ships were now required to take with them a reputable German inhabitant of Philadelphia versed in the English and German languages who was to act as interpreter He was to go aboard every vessel, call the passengers together and in a "loud and audible voice declare and proclaim" in the German language, the rights granted to passengers, by reading such passages of the law as pertains to their language.[8] To prevent the loss and confiscation of property, masters were required to give each passenger, sailing from any port of Europe, a bill of lading for all baggage not needed during the voyage, and this was to be carried in the same vessel occupied by the passenger to whom it belonged.

It has already been stated that the majority of vessels coming from the continent to America, were delayed at Great Britain, often several weeks, that the goods of passengers were there overhauled and duties collected thereon. This not only put the passengers to great inconveniences, causing a needless and expensive delay, but as many of the Germans were ignorant of the property subject to duties, their goods were often confiscated by the English custom house officials. To remedy this, masters of vessels were required to

---

[8] Act of the Assembly of the Province of Pennsylvania: 314. Phila., 1775.

pay all duties for the passengers, the amount of which was added to the regular fare.

An attempt to enforce the contract made between passengers and transporters in Europe, which had been so often disregarded, was also made at that time. It was now provided that 'every passenger who on landing paid the passage money contracted in Europe, shall be immediately discharged, and all his goods delivered on shore without further cost.' The same act provided that those not paying their freight at the port from which they sailed, were obliged to pledge their goods as lawful security for the payment of their passage. In case the goods were not of sufficient value to cover the fare, passengers were required to bind themselves as servants. No master of a vessel could collect the freight of a passenger who had died during the voyage, from his relatives; and no passenger could be compelled, against his will, to pay or make good by service all or any part of the freight of his relatives, except a man for his wife and children either dying during the voyage or actually transported. Children, whose father or mother did not survive the journey, might be held responsible for the freight of the parents by being compelled to serve until twenty-one years of age; and if they were of so advanced an age that the period of service, under these conditions, was not equal to the amount of the debt, the time of indenture could be extended, but not beyond the age of twenty-four years. Passengers unable to pay their freight might be kept on board thirty days after the vessel had arrived, but at the expense of the master or importer; the object of this was to give all passengers ample time to find relatives or friends who might wish to redeem them, or, to find suitable purchasers among strangers to whom they offered to bind themselves in return for the payment of their passage. If at the end of thirty days, passengers failed to find friends or purchasers to assume their debt, the expense of provisions was added to their fare.

Every indenture whereby passengers were bound was to be acknowledged before the Mayor or Recorder of Philadelphia, whose duty it was to keep an exact record, specifying "the Province, county, city, borough or township" where the master resided; "and the Mayor and Recorder and every Justice of the Peace in the several counties of this province in whose presence any assignment on such indenture may be made, shall in like manner keep a record of the place of the assignees abode." [*] No master or owner of any

---

[*] Acts of the Assembly of the Province of Pa., p. 316. Phila., 1775.

vessel could separate husband and wife, who came as passengers, by disposing them to different masters, except by mutual consent." [10]

The regulation of the passenger traffic was a gradual process which by no means approached perfection during the first century of the province of Pennsylvania. The successive acts of the Assembly were aimed against new abuses which crept into the system as immigration increased. The law of 1765 was the most elaborate and complete that had been passed up to that time, and formed the basis of all legislation relating to the control of the traffic during the later history of Pennsylvania, even after it became a state. Another act was passed in 1774 "to prevent infectious diseases being brought into the province;" it containing, however, nothing which had not been covered by previous acts, but imposing heavier penalties for the neglect of those sections which had in previous laws been violated.[11] From this act it appears that the sick on board the ships had frequently been concealed from the health officers, for which offence a penalty of 100 pounds was imposed for every one concealed.

The Revolution wrought few changes in the laws governing the transportation or conduct of servants. Those passed by the General Assembly of the Commonwealth were based as a rule on the Provincial Acts. A law of 1785, however, shows that the municipal government of Philadelphia where the majority of servants landed, had slightly changed, involving a change of functions in certain offices. Certain duties relating to servants formerly performed by the Mayor and Recorder now devolved upon the Justices of the Peace collectively or upon any three of them; such for example, as the registration of passengers. No provision had thus far been made for registering the names and acknowledging the indentures of German passengers separately. A new officer was now created, called the Register of German Passengers. He was to be appointed from time to time by the President in council, and placed under oath by the Chief Justice of the United States; his duties were to register all German passengers arriving in the city of Philadelphia and to execute all indentures; he must be an inhabitant of Philadelphia, speak the German and English languages with ease and propriety; by virtue of his office he could exercise all the power and authority of a Justice of the Peace so far as that power pertained to

---

[10] Ibid. This act was passed May 18, 1765.

[11] Acts of the Assembly of the Province of Pennsylvania, 505-507. Phila., 1775.

regulating and judging of the law respecting German passengers. The Health officer, having received from the Captain of any vessel importing German passengers the list of their names, was required to review them and report to the Register who, if he approved of their landing, sent the original list to the secretary of the Supreme Executive Council giving orders to land all passengers that were "sound and without defect in mind or body." All indentures and all assignments of Germans within Philadelphia were now to be acknowledged before the Register who made an entry of the transaction, and performed the work that had formerly been done by the Mayor or Recorder.[12] These entries are preserved in two manuscript volumes covering the period from 1786 to 1831, and are the most important source of information on the system of indentured service.

The last law relating to passengers was enacted by the Senate and House of Representatives of the Commonwealth of Pennsylvania in 1818. This act still recognizes the system of indentured service. Every passenger who offers to the master, captain, owner or consignee of the ship "the full sum for which he or she agreed in Europe, either in the coin or specie mentioned in the contract, or in lawful money of the United States equivalent thereto, and the fee of one dollar (provided by health law) * * * * shall be immediately discharged from such vessel and have all his or her goods delivered to them. * * * * But it shall be lawful for the master, importing passengers * * * * to keep and detain any such passengers who are unable to pay their freight * * * * for the space of thirty days next after their arrival * * * * in order that they may discharge their freight, or to agree with some person who shall be willing to pay the same in consideration of their servitude for a term of years." [13] No master or captain could make any contract with the passengers, compelling them to pay for the freight of another, unless they were both willing to enter into joint obligation. In case any action was brought by the redemptioners or other passengers against the importers, arising from the freight or passage, a speedy trial was guaranteed. Judges of the courts of the Commonwealth were, upon application by plaintiff, compelled to grant special courts and immediately decide causes.[14]

---

[12] Laws of the Commonwealth of Pa. II: 326-7. Phila., 1797.

[13] Acts of the General Assembly of the Commonwealth of Pa. p. 66. Harrisburg, 1818.

[14] Acts of the General Assembly of the Commonwealth of Pa. p 66. Harrisburg, 1818.

By the beginning of the present century the laws regulating transportation fairly accomplished the purpose of their creation. It must not, however, be assumed that they completely corrected the evils against which they were directed at any time during the period of indentured service. So long as the laws permitted the importer to hold servants for debts contracted on the voyage, every possible obstacle was thrown in the way of freedom. The profits arising from servants being much greater than those arising from the freemen, self interest directed the merchants to perpetuate the institution as long as possible, and not until a law was passed preventing imprisonment for debt did the merchants and importers lose their grip on this most lucrative traffic.

CHAPTER VII.

THE INDENTURE.

The relation of master and servant was founded on, or arising out of, the voluntary contract of two parties. This contract which was called an "indenture" specified the reciprocal rights and obligations of the master and servant. While the detailed specifications were not uniform in all contracts, the legal relations were essentially the same throughout the history of Pennsylvania both as a province and a state while the institution of indentured service was in operation.

In the ordinary indenture one party in consideration of a sum of money, which in the case of immigrants was paid for their passage to America, promises to bind himself for a definite period, as a servant to the debtor, who becomes master upon the signing of the contract. During the period specified in the indenture the servant promises to serve his master "honestly and obediently in all things as a good and faithful servant ought to do." The master on the other hand is under obligations to provide for the servant during the time of indenture, food, clothing, and lodging, and, at the expiration of the term, "freedom dues," which varied in different contracts but in nearly every case included among other things,"two complete suits of clothes," one of which was to be new.[1]

It must not be assumed that the money paid for the passage formed the only consideration for which servants were bound by indenture. It is true that the majority of servants came from that class of immigrants who were unable or unwilling to pay their passages; but many indentures were issued to those residing in the province, in which the consideration was an item of the future, either a sum of money or its equivalent. In an indenture dated May 19th, 1824, "Susanna Herbster of her own free will, and consent of her father," binds herself servant to Christian Schenck, for six years in consideration of "sufficient Drink, Apparel, Washing and lodging," including "six months' schooling;" in addition to this, certain privileges are specified in the indenture; the master within the first three years of the term of service is "to have her confirmed at the German

---

[1] See Appendix. I-II.

Lutheran Church in Philadelphia, and attend the Lectures of the minister agreeable to the form of said Church." At the expiration of her term of service she is to receive, "two complete suits of clothes, also a good bed, Bolster, Pillows and Blankets worth at least twenty-five Dollars." [2]

The "freedom dues" to which every servant was entitled, were provided for by law in case they were not mentioned in the indenture. Those servants who came with the first settlers of Pennsylvania received 50 acres of land, and usually a "years provision of Corn." [3] In New Jersey the "Grants and Concessions" of 1682 provided that if the freedom dues were not stipulated in the indenture each servant was to receive at the expiration of his term, "Ten bushels of corn, necessary apparel, two horses and one Axe." In 1700 an act of the Assembly of Pennsylvania provided that "every servant that shall faithfully serve, four years or more, shall at the expiration of their servitude, have a discharge, and shall be duly clothed with two Compleat Suits of Apparel, whereof one shall be new, and shall also be furnished with one Axe, one Grubbing hoe, and one Weeding-hoe, at the charge of their master or mistress." [4] A modification of this act, in which that portion relating to the implements was repealed, was made in 1771. After this the "customary freedom dues" were two complete suits of clothes, though frequently other articles were added depending entirely on the agreement of the contracting parties. After the revolution a money payment was often added to the regular dues, and sometimes substituted entirely for them. [5]

---

[2] Ibid.

[3] In 1693 a servant complained that he had been turned off "without clothes fitting for a servant to have." The Court ordered his master to "pay him a hat, coat, waistcoat, breeches, drawers, stockings, and shoes, all new, and also ten bushels of wheat or fourteen bushels of corn, two hoes and One Axe." Such complaints were common and were called claims "for the Custom of the County." Hist. of Delaware Co. p. 186. Phila., 1862.

[4] Acts of the Assembly of the Province of Pennsylvania. p. 7. Phila., 1775.

In Maryland a law of 1715 provided the following freedom dues: "Every man servant shall have at the Expiration of servitude, 1 new Hat, 1 good suit, (coat and breeches) either Kersey or broad-cloth, 1 new shirt of white linen, 1 pair of French Fall Shoes, and stockings, 2 houghs (hoes) and 1 Axe, 1 gun, value 20s. Women Servants: Waste Coat and Petty coat of new half thick or penistone, a new shift of white linen (Two suits), Shoes and Stockings, a blue apron, Two caps of white linen, and 3 barrels of Indian corn."—A Complete Collection of the Laws of Md. 1692-1725, Annapolis, 1727.

[5] See Appendix. III.

The original act providing for the freedom dues gave no express authority to the courts for the delivery and payment of the same. As a result many were discharged at the end of their service without receiving them, and as the action for recovery was attended with much expense and trouble the majority thus wronged were discouraged from prosecuting their suits and thus deprived of their just dues. To remedy this an act was passed in 1771, establishing an easy method for servants to secure their rights; a justice of any county within the province on complaint made by a servant, could summon the master before him and order him to pay the "just dues to the servant according to law and Indenture." [6]

The time of service in Pennsylvania varied more than in any other colony; on an average, however, the terms were shorter than in other colonies. In New Jersey the early laws fixed the term of all servants above the age of twenty-one, at four years, the term to begin "from the time the ship shall be entered in the said Province." In Maryland an act of 1671 fixes the time of all servants above 22 years of age at five years; if between eighteen and twenty-two, six years; all those between fifteen and eighteen were required to serve until twenty-two years of age.[7] Seven years of service was frequent in Massachusetts, and in Rhode Island ten years were sometimes required of adults. The early laws of Pennsylvania required of those without indenture a term of four years; but in the majority of cases the time was specified in the indenture and was more often below four years than above. The time depended upon the age, strength, and health of those sold. Children above five years of age usually had to serve until they had attained the age of twenty-one; those under five, could not be sold and were usually disposed of gratuitously to persons who kept them until at twenty-one years of age, they were set at liberty. As children were often required to assume the passage dues of parents their time of service was sometimes extended beyond the age of twenty-one.[8]

One of the duties of the county court was to determine the age of children and the time they were to serve. This was called "Judging" them. A record of the court of Delaware County, in the October session of 1693, makes mention of "the eight boys that

---

[6] Acts of the Assembly of the Province of Pa. p. 392. Phila., 1775.

[7] Md. Archives and Acts of the Assembly 1666-76. p. 335. Baltimore, 1884.

[8] The time of service of immigrants is given in detail in a preceding Chapter on "The Voyage."

Morris Trent brought into the country, who were called up to be judged." They were ordered to serve their respective masters until they arrived at the age of twenty-one.[9] Seven years later in the Chester County Court, "Francis Chadsey brought a boy who was adjudged to serve eight years, to be taught to read and write, or else to serve but seven years." The same master "also had a servant maid who was adjudged to serve five years."[10] During the same session "a servant girl who was adjudged to be eleven years of age" was ordered to serve "Thomas Withers or his assigns ten years."[11] Frequently whole families bound themselves to the same master. A single example of the many entries from the Registry of Redemptioners will serve as an illustration: "Conrad Rihl and Wife, Catharina Elizabeth, as also their son by their Consent, named George Herman, bound themselves to Andrew Porter of Montgomery County near Norris Town, the Parents Three years each, to have customary freedom suits each; their son George Herman, to serve Twelve years, to have customary freedom suits, to learn to read, write and cypher; their child Catharina Elizabeth to be free when the parents are free."[12]

A servant binding himself by indenture could by virtue of the contract, be sold to another master in the Province. In a transfer of this kind, the terms of the indenture had to be carried out by the new purchaser. An act of 1729 provides for the method by which sales were to be made in the city of Philadelphia, which will serve as an example for the whole Province. "All assignments or sales of servants shall be made before the Mayor, or in case of his absence before the Recorder." These officers were to keep a record of the names of the servants, "by whom and to whom assigned, and the term of years mentioned in the indenture." After the creation of the office of Registry of German Passengers in 1785, the assignment of all German passengers, was executed before the Register, while that of other immigrants was executed by the Justice of the Peace, the offices of Mayor and Recorder having changed in names and functions.[13]

The record of the Upland County Court from 1676 to 1681 be-

[9] History of Delaware County.

[10] Quoted in Hist. of Chester Co.: 430. Phila., 1881.

[11] Ibid, p. 431.

[12] MSS., Registry of Redemptioners, in Hist. Soc. of Penn. Dated March 30, 1795.

[13] Acts of Assembly of the Province of Pa. p. 162. Phila., 1775.

fore the organization of Pennsylvania into a Proprietary Government, shows that a regular method of assignment had at that time already been established, and that the practice of selling the time of servants was not uncommon at this early date. An entry dated March 12, 1678, reads: "Anthony Long brought in Court a certayne man servant named William Goaf whome hee has bought of Moens Peterson for the full term of Three years servitude. The s'd Wm. Goaf being present in court did owne the same, and did faithfully promise to serve his master honestly and truly ye above s'd Term of Three years." [14] Such sales were more frequent in the latter part of the eighteenth and the beginning of the nineteenth century. In 1792 Anna Ballman bound herself for three and a half years; within the first year of her indenture she had served five different masters. [15]

In the newspapers of the time frequent advertisements are found like the following from the Pennsylvania Packet, dated October 25th, 1773: "A strong hearty woman servant, who has about two years and a half to serve, very suitable for the Country." [16] The fact that servants sometimes voluntarily bound themselves a second time, after the first indenture had expired, indicates that their condition under indenture, was, during the latter part of the 18th century rather mild. The practice of servants binding themselves a second term was not uncommon in Pennsylvania. An example of this is found in John Hesselbach and his wife who bind themselves in 1784 to a Philadelphia merchant. Four years later they again voluntarily bind themselves to an iron master of Chester County for four years. [17] That their condition at this time differed little from the "hired servant" who was under no contract, is also shown from the fact that frequently the indenture mentions in addition to "freedom dues," a definite sum of money, which omitted would shorten the time of service.

It thus appears that the system is gradually changing from one of forced service on account of debt, to a free and natural method of employment. The long term service, as opposed to hire by the year, had its advantages to employers and employed. An indenture

---

[14] Record of Upland Court in Penn. 1676-81, p. 89. Phila., 1860.

[15] Registry of Redemptioners. MSS.

[16] On the same page is the following: "To be sold: The time of an Irish Servant woman, who has three and a half years to serve, fit for either town or country. Enquire of the Printer."

[17] Registry of Redemptioners. MSS. Dec. 15, 1784, and Sept. 10, 1788.

of four years relieved the servant of all responsibility to provide for himself during that period, and whatever misfortune might beset him, during that time he was sure of the stipulations mentioned in the contract, if he performed the ordinary duties devolved upon him as a servant. To foreigners to be assured of the necessaries of life for a definite number of years, in a country with whose laws and customs they were unfamiliar, must have been a relief from much anxiety. During this period they become acquainted with the manners and customs of the country, and when their time of service had expired, they were fitted for duties of everyday life. The masters, on the other hand, were likewise benefitted by the long term of employment, for since the development of natural resources in the absence of modern machinery was almost entirely dependent upon manual labor, and since there was almost always an under supply of labor steady service could hardly have been secured without long contracts. There was also by the system of indenture a political advantage shared by the Province and Commonwealth of no small consequence: viz., the temporary disfranchisement of the servants, who constituted, as has been shown, a large part of the foreign population, gave ample opportunity to prepare them for citizenship.[18]

---

[18] J. C. Ballagh, White Servitude in the Colony of Va. Johns Hopkins University Studies. Vol. XIII: p. 90, note.

CHAPTER VIII.

THE "RUNAWAYS."

The "Great Law" passed at Chester in 1682 provides "that no master or mistress or freeman of the Province or the Territories thereunto belonging, shall presume to sell or dispose of any servant into any other Province." This law was abrogated in 1693, under William and Mary, but it was the basis of similar laws which were later passed, and contains essentially the regulations in operation through the greater part of the Colonial period. The demand for laborers and the desire to retain them was no doubt the controlling reason in Penn's mind for enacting laws to prevent servants leaving the Province. The attempt to keep all the servants within the Province was indeed a large undertaking, too great to be successful. That this act was frequently violated is shown by the numerous petitions from masters of servants, and from the various county courts, to the provincial council. One from the court of Philadelphia was sent to that body in 1685, stating that several servants were brought from England to "serve in this province, and that the masters of the vessels intended to carry them to Virginia," contrary to the laws of the province.[1] Further provisions were made against servants' leaving the province by a law of the Assembly in 1700. It is evident from this act, and from the frequent complaints found in contemporary documents, that the settlers in other provinces often gave encouragement to servants to leave their original masters by offering easier conditions, such for example as a shorter term of service than the original indenture called for; many escaped to other provinces to avoid justice; sometimes masters sold servants into another province against their will.

The rendition of fugitives from one colony to another was a frequent source of annoyance to the colonial governments. As early as 1643, e. g., the council of Maryland sent a letter to the Governor of New Netherlands asking the return of servants who had escaped from Maryland.[2] In the absence of inter-colonial regulations, providing for the return of fugitives, an act was passed in 1700, to pre-

---

[1] Colonial Records I: 161.

[2] Proceedings of the Council of Maryland, 1636-47: p. 134. Baltimore, 1885.

vent and discourage servants' leaving the province of Pennsylvania,
providing "that no servant bound to serve in this province, or Counties annexed, shall be sold or disposed of to any person residing in
any other Province or government, without the consent of the servant, and two Justices of the Peace of the county wherein he lives
or is sold, under the penalty of 10 pounds to be forfeited by the
seller." [3]

In order to discourage piracies and robberies an act was passed
in the same year which affected runaway servants,—in fact every one
leaving the province: "All unknown persons coming to lodge or
sojourn in an inn, or ask for work * * * * in any kind of a
house, and cannot give a good account of themselves and their former and present way of living, and have not a pass under hand and
seal of at least one Justice of the Peace, stating whence they came
from and their destination * * * * shall be taken up as a sus-
pect criminal." [4] Five years later this law was abrogated, but similar regulations existed throughout the colonial period. [5]

A further precaution was early taken to prevent fugitive servants from leaving the province by an act requiring every person
intending to leave, to publish his intention in writing and affix it to
the door of the County Court, thirty days before departing. Masters of vessels who attempted to take any one out of the province
without leave, were to pay all damage incurred by such transgres-
sion, and every master importing servants was to give a bond of 300
pounds to the naval officers to observe the laws, twenty pounds to
be forfeited for every violation. [6]

---

[3] Acts of the Assembly of the Province of Pa.: 7, Phila., 1775.

[4] Statutes at Large of Pa. II: 102, 1896.

[5] As early as 1672 in Upland County the following regulations existed:
"Whereas frequent complaints have been made of servants who run away
from their masters in other governments, for want of due care and examina-
tion of them by the magistrates or officers of the towns through which they
pass, It is ordered that if hereafter any stranger or person unknown shall
come to, or travaill through any town or place within this government without a passport or certificate from whence he came and whither he is bound,
shall be liable to be seized upon by any officers of the town or place into
which he comes, or through which he shall travel, there to be secured until
he can clear himselfe to bee a freeman, and shall defray the charges of his
detention there, by his work or labor (if not otherwise able to give satisfaction) in the best way and manner he shall bee found capable."—Dukes'
Laws. Coll. N. Y. Hist. Soc. I: 421.

[6] Passed Nov. 27, 1700.—Statutes at Large of Pa. II: 84. 1896. The pro-
totype of this act is found in Penn's "Concessions to the Province of Pa.,"

In consequence of these laws which existed in nearly all of the colonies travellers without passes were in constant anxiety of being apprehended as runaways. In 1723, Franklin in his Autobiography, speaking of his journey from New York to Philadelphia says, "I stopped at a poor inn where I stayed all night ✳ ✳ ✳ ✳ I made so miserable a figure, too, that I found, by the questions asked me, I was suspected to be some runaway indentured servant, and in danger of being taken up on that suspicion." Again after arriving at Philadelphia and being directed to a "house where they receive strangers" he writes, "while I was eating, several questions were asked me as, from my youth and appearance, I was suspected of being a runaway." [']

The question of runaway servants seemed to have been one of the most difficult with which the authorities and masters had to deal. The Pennsylvania newspapers of the time devoted no small amount of space to notices of runaways. It is difficult to find a single issue of the *Packet* or *Gazette* during the period in which the system was in full force, that does not contain several notices, and sometimes over a column is devoted to these advertisements. "Runaway from his Master," "Forty Shillings Reward," "Twenty Hard Dollars Reward," "A Half Johannes Reward," are some of the various captions that stand out in boldface type to attract the notice of the reader. Rough wood cuts were sometimes inserted beside the notice to make it more conspicuous, the fugitive being usually represented in colonial costume with a cane and bundle over his shoulder taking rapid strides across the country. These notices throw a great deal of light on the internal history of indentured service. They give a complete description of the servant, his character, nationality, age, the clothing and often the time of service. As the reurn of the servant depended largely upon the accuracy of the description, it is an invaluable source from which a perfect picture of the dress, manner, and character, of at least a part of the servant class, may be derived. A single example from the Pennsylvania

---

1681, section XX: "That no person leave the province without publication being made thereof in the market place, three weeks before, and a certificate from some Justice of the Peace of his clearness with his neighbors and those he dealt with, so far as such assurance can be given, and if any master of a ship shall, contrary hereunto, receive and carry away any person, that hath not given that public notice, the said master shall be liable to all debts owing by said person, so secretly transported from the province."—Charters and Constitutions of the U. S.

['] Autobiography Chap. II.

6

Gazette of May 9, 1751, may here serve as a characteristic illustration: "Run away from Thomas James, of Upper Merion, Philadelphia County, on the 5th of this inst, an Irish servant lad named William Dobbin, about 18 years of age, speaks good English, fresh colour'd, thick and well set in his body, has light colored curled hair, some what resembling a wig; Had on when he went away, an old felt hat, ozenbrigs shirt, an old dark brown colour'd coat, too big for him, and breeches of the same, grey worsted stockings, and a pair of old shoes, with brass buckles, one of the buckles broke. Whoever takes up and seizes this servant so that his master may have him again, shall have 20 shillings reward, and reasonable charges, paid by Thomas Jones." To this is added the following postscript: "He often changes his clothes and sometimes gets them without money."[1] On at least one occasion a runaway was the inspiration of a poetic attempt as the following from the Maryland Gazette under the heading of "Forty Shillings Reward" will show:

> "Last Wednesday noon at break of day,
> From Philadelphia ran away
> An Irishman named John McKeohn,
> To fraud and imposition prone;
> About five feet, five inches high,
> Can curse and swear as well as lie;
> How old he is I can't engage
> But fourty-five is near his age.
> He came (as all reports agree)
> From Belfast town in sixty-three."

In the same strain the features, speech and dress are described and then continues,

> "He oft in conversation chatters
> Of scripture and religious matters,
> And fain would to the world impart
> That virtue lodges in his heart;
> But take the rogue from stem to stern,
> The hypocrite you'll soon discern—
> And find (tho' his deportment's civil)
> A saint without, within a devil.
> Whoe'er secures said John McKeohn,
> (Provided I can get my own),
> Shall have from me, in cash paid down,
> Five dollar bills, and half a crown,"[2]

---

[1] A number of these notices are given in Appendix V.
[2] Md. Gazette, Mch. 16, 1769. Quoted in Scharf's Hist. of Md. II: 17n.

In spite of the severe laws and precautionary measures, such as requiring all travelers to have passes, fugitive servants seemed to have been very successful in eluding detection. Frequently they secured passes, issued to another person whose name they assumed, to prevent being caught.[10] Sometimes they escaped from on board the ship before being sold. Under these conditions, as no record could be made of their arrival and they could easily find friends who would shield them in return for services on easy conditions, it was comparatively easy to avoid detection. Many schemes were practiced by fugitives to evade the laws. In a notice of a runaway dated March 17, 1752, a servant under his second indenture "is supposed to have his old indenture with him" which seems to have been equivalent to a pass. Another of the preceding year "had a pass from his master to go to Philadelphia on the 19th instant to return the 26th, which it is supposed he altered."

The great majority of runaways were Irish and English; but few notices are found in which the names are German.[11] Those that came from England as servants were composed, to a considerable extent, of that shiftless population so numerous in the large cities of England during the colonial period. It was this class which gave the courts the greatest employment and filled the newspapers of the time with notices of runaways. While the Germans on the other hand had also the reckless and adventurous among their numbers, they came as a rule from that class who sought to better their condition by labor, and to establish homes. They were also an industrious class which formed the backbone of the agricultural interests of the colony. Further, even though among a large number of their countrymen, they were nevertheless in an English colony, and an attempt at runaway was naturally attended with greater risk to one to whom the laws and customs of the country were foreign.

Many laws were passed to prevent servants' leaving their masters, and every possible encouragement was given to citizens to ap-

---

[10] "Runaway on the first Day of July last, from William Wright of Lancaster County a servant man named Thomas McSwine, but goes by the name of Thomas McGill, having with him a pass that belonged to one of that name."—Pa. Gazette, Mch. 20, 1740.

[11] In New Jersey where the population and condition of servants were not unlike those of Pennsylvania, out of 165 runaways advertised in the various newspapers during the period from 1751 to 1755, it appears that 60 were Irish; 30 negroes (slaves); 22 English; 16 Dutch; 5 Scotch; 2 Welsh; 2 French; of the remaining 28, there was no means of determining the nationality.—New Jersey Archives, First series, Vol. XIX.

prehend fugitives and deliver them over to the authorities. In 1683 a bill was proposed by the Governor and passed by the council providing that servants who ran away from their masters should serve five days for every day absent during the time of their service, and pay the costs and damages caused by their absence.[12] In 1700 the Assembly enacted a law offering ten shillings reward to any one who "shall apprehend or take up any runaway servant, and shall bring him or her to the sheriff of the county." This amount was paid by the sheriff, if the runaway was taken up within ten miles of the servant's abode. It was the duty of the sheriff to send notice to the master or owner, of whom he was to receive five shillings as prison fees upon the delivery of the servant," together with other "Disbursements and reasonable charges for and upon the same." All expenses incurred by the absence were finally to be paid by the runaway either by an extension of the time of service, or in money.[13] A common practice which encouraged servants to leave their master was the secret employment of runaways by employers who offered to the fugitives easier conditions than those stipualted in their original indenture. The new master would offer to shorten the time of service, to keep the fugitive concealed, to pay money for his services, and to make other concessions if necessary. He might even offer him the terms of an ordinary hired servant, thus restoring him to freedom. To those servants who felt themselves oppressed by their masters, the offer of money wages and liberty was indeed a strong temptation, and it is not strange that many risked the penalty to gain their freedom, consequently an act was passed in the same year providing that "whoever shall conceal any servant or entertain him twenty-four hours without his master's consent, and shall not within the said time give notice thereof to some Justice of the Peace of the county, shall forfeit twenty shillings for every day's concealment." The Justice was compelled to issue a warrant within twenty-four hours after being notified to the next constable who was to commit the fugitive to the custody of the sheriff, who, after receiving him, was to notify the owner or master.[14] It would be erroneous to suppose that these laws against runaways were not frequently violated, for the operation of an institution cannot always be determined by the laws which are made to govern it. Especially was this true in the case of indentured servants. The law passed in

[12] Col. Records, I: 80.
[13] Acts of the Assembly of the Province of Pa.: p. 8. Phila., 1775.
[14] Acts of Assembly of Province of Pa. p. 8. Phila., 1775.

1700 concerning runaways was frequently violated and frequent amendments were called for. This is shown by the preamble to an act of 1771 which recites that doubts have arisen whether after the expiration of the time of service justices can order servants, who during their time of service quitted their master, to make up lost time. Evidently the framers of the old law presupposed that all cases arising from runaways would be settled during the time of indenture; that fugitives could not avoid detection for a long time. The actual conditions, however, proved to be quite the contrary; many servants who ran away from their masters succeeded in avoiding detection; the court records show comparatively few cases where the servant's time was extended for running away, and it may therefore safely be inferred that the majority were never returned to their original owners. To settle all doubts as to previous laws it was now enacted that Justices of the Peace upon application or complaint of the master could oblige a person to make full recompense for the damages and charges sustained by his absence as a servant, either by serving five days for every day's absence, or by other satisfaction as the justice should decide.[15] This act was important as it made all of those liable to service, who at any time previously engaged as servants, had left their masters. In other words, a servant remained as such until he had served out the term of indenture regardless of the number of years he had been away from his master. In 1713 the General Assembly of New Jersey passed a law providing that servants absenting themselves from their masters without leave, were to serve double the time of their absence, and pay all costs incurred in their return. The same law also made it a penalty for any one to advise a servant to run away; ten shillings being the fine for every day's concealment, and a reward of fifteen shillings was promised to any who would apprehend or return a runaway. Here, as in Pennsylvania, a pass was required of all travellers, and boatmen and tavern-keepers were warned against carrying or entertaining suspected fugitives.[16]

In Maryland the regulations to prevent runaways were much the same as in Pennsylvania, though the penalties for their violation were much more severe. An act was passed in that province in 1692, providing that all servants, even those hired for wages, trav-

---

[15] Acts of the Assembly of the Province of Pennsylvania: 392. Philadelphia, 1775.
[16] Acts of the General Assembly of the Province of New Jersey, 1702-1776. Burlington, 1776.

elling ten miles from the house of their masters, should have a note
under the hand of their overseer on penalty of being taken up for
a runaway; it further provided that any servant absenting himself
should serve ten days for every day's absence; that any who entertained a runaway, should pay a fine of 500 pounds of tobacco for
every twenty-four hours' entertainment; that all persons travelling
outside of the County in which they resided, should have a pass
under the seal of the County. Twenty pounds of tobacco were given
as a reward for taking up runaways. The Indians, even, were
encouraged in hunting down fugitives and delivering them to a
magistrate by being rewarded for their services by the gift of a
"Match Coat" or the value of one.[17] A supplement to this act was
passed in 1719 providing for the disposal of fugitives who were in
charge of the sheriff; if a master neglected to redeem him after
receiving notice of his seizure, by paying all charges, the sheriff
could sell him, retain his own fees, and be accountable to the owner
for the residue.[18] That a similar law was in operation in Pennsylvania is shown from the advertisement of a certain William Strand,
keeper of the prison at Norristown. The notice is in the Pennsylvania Packet of October 7, 1789, and reads as follows: "Was committed to the gaol of Montgomery County, a certain George Sharpe,
who says he is a servant to Patrick Story, in Sussex County, State
of New Jersey, His master is desired to take him away in three
weeks from the date or he will be sold for his fees." [19]

In some of the colonies cruel treatment on the part of the
masters, was doubtless the cause of many runaways. In Maryland
for example, a certain Richard Garford testified in a case brought
before the Provincial Court in 1656, that "he was employed by John
Little to fetch home his servant Billsberry and his Indian from the
Indian cabin and they would not come saying they would rather
live with pagans than to come home to be starved for want of food
and to have their brains beaten out." [20] Complaints of cruel treatment were not infrequently brought before the Provincial Courts of
Maryland. The case referred to, however, was an extreme example,
and it would be incorrect to assume from individual cases that such

---

[17] Maryland Archives; Proceedings and Acts of the Assembly; 1684-92;
p. 451ff. Baltimore, 1894.

[18] A Compleat Collection of the Laws of Maryland; 1692-1725; p. 209.

[19] History of Montgomery County: 299. Phila., 1884.

[20] Md. Archives, Judicial and Testamentary Business of the Provincial
Court, 1649-'57: p. 484; Baltimore, 1891.

was the general rule of their treatment. It depended entirely upon the master and the servant. In many instances harsh treatment was justified. In 1654 a suit was brought before the same court by a master against his two Irish servants for absenting themselves "for a long time" from service. The servants maintained that the cause of their leaving was abuse from the master in giving correction. "It appeared to the Court that the correction was not given without just cause. They were absent about six weeks." The court decided that for the expense incurred by their absence they were to pay 200 pounds of tobacco, and serve eight months in addition to the full time of indenture.[31]

The treatment of servants in Pennsylvania was better than in Maryland and perhaps better than in any other colony; and the reason for the large number of runaways finds its explanation in other causes than cruel treatment. The servants who came to Pennsylvania may be divided into two classes; first those who came to the colony with a sincere desire to better their condition, to establish homes for themselves and their children, by honest labor; these gave little or no trouble, and usually served out their time to the satisfaction of their masters; the other class were such as had been deceived by enchanting stories of fabulous wealth and fortunes that they supposed awaited them on their arrival. When indolence failed to bring the promised reward, when they realized that four years of monotonous labor under a stern master yielded only the bare necessities of life, they were disappointed and sought every opportunity to flee from a service that to them seemed worse than "Egyptian bondage." Among this class were also the shiftless who came from the English cities, sent to the colony to prevent them from becoming criminals at home. With no fixed purpose in life, with an abhorrence for labor, with a disregard for law and discipline, they were in disposition what they had been at home—vagabonds, and became in the colony the troublesome "runaways."

[31] Md. Archives, Judicial and Testamentary Business of the Provincial Court, 1649-'57; p. 396. Baltimore, 1891.

CHAPTER IX.

PUNITIVE AND MARRIAGE REGULATIONS.

A. PUNITIVE.

The ordinary penalty imposed upon runaway servants, as has been shown, was an extension of the time of service or the payment of a fine in money. But for these and other offences severer methods of punishing the recalcitrants were allowed in Pennsylvania from the time of its establishment as a proprietary colony to the end of the 18th century. Masters were given the power of corporal punishment and from the contemporary accounts there is reason to believe that this right was frequently exercised. In one of the early meetings of the Provincial council, held in 1683, William Penn "put the question whether a proclamation were not convenient to be put forth to Impower Masters to chastise their servants, and to punish any that shall Inveigle any servant to goe from his master." It was unanimously agreed to by the council,[1] and it may here be added, practiced by the masters throughout the colonial period.

The mode of punishment varied in different colonies and in different times. Whipping and confinement to the public work-house was the ordinary method employed in minor offences, and was usually resorted to as a substitute for an extension of service. The court records of 1671 of New Amsterdam contain a case which was rather unusual and may here be mentioned by way of comparison. A servant lad being imprisoned for stealing a ring, and refusing to tell where he concealed it, was ordered to be privately whipped. After this punishment, he still refused to disclose the stolen article. The court then ordered that a year be added to the time of his indenture, and that the master should have the liberty of selling him to Virginia or any other colony.[2] To sell offenders out of the province was an unique way of disposing of an objectionable class, and not usually practiced under any condition. On the contrary, each colony usually attempted to reform its own criminals, and the law of Pennsylvania especially provides that no offender can be sold out of the Province under any conditions.

---

[1] Colonial Records I: 79.
[2] Records of New Amsterdam 1653-74, VI: 279. N. Y., 1897.

The legal relation of white servants, negroes and Indian slaves, to the free population in Pennsylvania is shown to some extent by the penal laws and the methods of punishment prescribed to transgressors. In nearly all cases the punishment of freemen and servants differs, but in the majority of instances servants and slaves are classed in the same punitive category. An act of 1735, passed to prevent setting fires to woods, fixes the same penalty and mode of punishment for white servants as for negroes. "Any servant or negro slave," convicted of the violation of the act, "shall be whipped with any number of stripes not exceeding twenty-one, on his or her bare back, at the Discretion of the Justice * * * * and further, shall be committed to the Work-house of the county where the offence is committed, there to remain until the Costs of Prosecution shall be paid."[3] In this act it is also provided that the master could prevent the state from administering corporal punishment to his servant or slave by paying the damages incurred by the violation of the act.

In this connection it may be mentioned that in extreme offences against the state, freemen could under certain conditions, be sold into "servitude." A law passed by the Assembly in 1739 provides that any one convicted of forgery or counterfeiting any kind of money, shall be sentenced to the pillory, to have both ears cut off and nailed to the pillory, and to be whipped on the bare back with thirty-one lashes, "well laid on;" in addition to this, to forfeit the sum of 100 pounds to be levied on the goods and chattels of the offender; to pay the aggrieved double the value of the damage sustained, with the costs and charges of prosecution; if the offender was unable to pay the damages and charges, he could be sold into "servitude" not exceeding seven years.[4] "An act for regulating the nightly watch within the City of Philadelphia," passed by the Assembly in 1751, shows clearly the legal position of freemen, white servants and negroes with regard to punishment. For offences against this act, freemen were to pay five pounds for the first offence, and ten pounds for the second and every other offence; but "if any servant or negro slave be convicted of incurring any of the fines, * * * * he shall for the first offence be whipped on the bare back with twenty-one lashes at the public whipping post and kept on bread and water at hard labor in the public work-house three

---

[3] Acts of the Assembly of the Prov. of Pa.: 187. Phila., 1775.
[4] Statutes at Large of Pa. IV: 359,—1897.

days; and for the second and every other offence shall receive thirty-one lashes, and be kept six days at hard labor." In a statute passed five years later the same distinction is made between freeman and servants.[5] In these two laws negroes and white servants were classed alike in matters of punishment. No provision was here made by which the masters could prevent the prescribed punishment from being inflicted by paying the damage incurred by the servant, as was the case in many penal laws. Here there was no alternative for the offending servant—white or black—but the whipping post and confinement at hard labor.

On account of these differences in punishment, it does not, however, follow that the servant or slave was made the object of legal discrimination because of his inferior position in the social scale. As negroes were slaves for life no other than corporal punishment could well be applied. An offence committed by a slave incurring a loss to the state, must remain a loss, unless it was paid by the master; no extension of time as in the case of servants could be used as a compensative method of correction. In another act of 1751 against racing and gambling, without license from the government, servants, negroes, and Indian slaves are treated alike in the matter of punishment, which differs from that of freemen in being corporal instead of a fine in money. The penalty for a violation of the act by a freeman consisted in the payment of a fine of three pounds for the first offence, and five pounds for the second and every other offence; a violation of the same act by "a servant, or negro or Indian slave," was made punishable by fifteen lashes, applied in the usual manner, and six days' confinement at hard labor in the County Work house, for the first offence; and twenty-one lashes and ten days confinement for the second and every other offence.[6]

Although in some instances the punishment of servants was the same as that applied to negroes, and although it differed at times from that of freemen, it is not to be assumed that this was always the case. Many laws were common to freemen and servants. The peculiar relation of masters and servants necessitated certain special laws for the latter, just as minors to-day are subject to certain laws which apply to them alone. In some respects the legal relation of master and servant was like that of the parent and child. This relation is shown in an act of 1756 providing against the destruction of private and public property in the city of Philadel-

[5] Statutes at Large of Pa. V: 126, 241,—1898.
[6] Statutes at Large of Pennsylvania; V: 110. 1898.

phia: "If any person under age, bound servant, apprentice, negro or mulatto be convicted of incurring any penalties or damages mentioned in this act, the parent, guardian, or master shall be obliged to pay the said penalties in the same manner as if they themselves had been guilty of incurring the same." [1]

Generally speaking, the punishment of servants as provided by law was not unusually severe, when compared with that provided for the punishment of freemen. It would be incorrect to suppose that because servants were more frequently made to suffer corporal punishment than freemen, that there was any legal disparity between the two classes farther than that arising from the necessity of the relationship. In other words, there was no legal discrimination against servants. The general aim of the penal code in regard to servants was to make the offender financially responsible for all damages and charges incurred by the violation of an act. But as the servant was not supposed to possess the means of liquidating a fine by the payment of money, there was no alternative but to extend the time of service or to apply corporal punishment. For example, in case of a runaway, who had been taken up and returned to his master, the fees of the notice, of the constable, of the sheriff, the reward, though paid directly by the master, were ultimately paid by the servant in an extension of the time of service. Ordinarily in civil offences the time was extended; in criminal offences, corporal punishment and confinement in the public work-house were demanded by the state, unless the master paid the damage incurred by his servant, which, as has been shown, was permitted in some instances.

The severity of the penal laws, affecting servants, must be considered in the light of the conditions and times in which they were framed. Among the more unusual punishments applied to freemen, whipping was common, and is even practiced to-day in some of the states; branding, gagging, wearing the badge of thievery, the pillory, "to have the ears cut off and nailed to the pillory," were punishments prescribed by the law; lying in common conversation cost a half crown or three days' imprisonment, if the laws were enforced. The whipping of a woman servant had a parallel in the custom law on the statute books even to the end of the 18th century, which "allowed men to beat their wives with a stick, provided it was not bigger than the judge's thumb." [2] As late as 1783 the court of

---

[1] Statutes at Large of Pa. V: 241. 1898.
[2] Hist. of Westmoreland County (Pa.): 59. Phila., 1882.

Westmoreland county records a sentence of a most barbarous nature: A certain John Smith pleads guilty to the crime of felony and this judgment is rendered: "that the said John Smith be taken to-morrow morning * * * * to the public whipping post and there to receive thirty-nine lashes on his bare back, well laid on; that his ears be cut off and nailed to the common pillory; that he stand one hour in the pillory; that he make restitution of the stolen goods; that he pay a fine of twenty pounds * * * * and that he stand committed until this sentence is complied with." [9]

Trade with servants was prohibited by an act of the Assembly in 1700. The object of this law was to prevent a practice which seems to have been very common in some of the colonies: The court records and contemporary documents show that frequent complaints were filed against servants for stealing their masters' goods which they sold to persons who made a practice of this illicit trade. The desire for ready money on the part of the servant was a strong incentive leading him to accept the offer of the illegal purchasers, who in some cases seem to have carried on an extensive and systematic trade. To discourage this trade it was enacted, "that whosoever shall deal or traffick with any servant, white or black, for any kind of goods or Merchandise without leave of the owner * * * * shall forfeit treble the value of the goods to the owner; and the servant if white, shall make satisfaction to his master by servitude, after the expiration of the time of service, to double the value of the goods; if black, shall be severely whipped in the most public place of the township where the offence is committed." [10]

An act of 1721 places the servant in the same legal category as the minor. It forbids innkeepers within the province from receiving, harboring, entertaining or trusting any minor under 21 years of age; or any servant knowing them to be such, or being warned against it by the master. The penalty imposed upon the innkeeper for the violation of this act was the same whether in connection with a minor or servant. [11]

B. MARRIAGE.

In regard to marriage the master occupied a position which, in its relation to the servant, was not unlike that existing between parent and child. In 1701 the assembly passed a law fixing the con-

---

[9] Quoted in Hist. of Westmoreland Co. (Pa.): 59. Phila., 1882.
[10] Acts of the Assembly of the Province of Pa.: 8. Phila., 1775.
[11] Laws of the Commonwealth of Pa. I: 156. Phila., 1797.

ditions under which a servant might marry. Any servant marrying
without the consent of the master or mistress was required to serve
one year after the regular time of service had expired. Any free
man marrying a servant without the consent of the master was
required to pay twelve pounds or perform one year's service; if a
free woman married a servant under the same conditions she was
required to pay six pounds, or serve one year. The conditions
imposed upon a servant marrying without the consent of the master
were the same whether the marriage was with a servant or with a
free person—in each case a year was added to the time of service.[12]
Those servants who belonged to religious societies were not
included in this act, and might marry in the society to which they
belonged, provided either party to the marriage gave notice to the
master a month before the marriage was solemnized. As no penalty
was imposed upon the justices of the peace for marrying persons
contrary to this law it was frequently eluded until in 1730, a fine of
fifty pounds was imposed upon any officer uniting in marriage any
persons not possessing the proper credentials.[13] The right on the
part of the servant to marry involved a penalty which was ordinarily
so far beyond his means that the master virtually had the power of
prohibiting the marriage of any servant without his consent. He
might ask any price not exceeding twelve pounds, in the case of
men, and six pounds in the case of women; or demand from each
an additional year of labor.[14]

As the negroes constituted a comparatively small part of the
servant class in Pennsylvania there seems to have been little occasion for laws regulating the marriage between whites and slaves.
The nearest approach to such a law was an act of the Assembly in

---

[12] Acts of the Assembly of the Province of Pa.: 18. Phila., 1775.

[13] Statutes at Large of Pennsylvania; IV: 154. 1897.

Abbé Raynal in speaking of the servants in Pennsylvania says: "None of
those who are contracted for, have a right to marry without the approbation
of their master, who sets what price he choses on his consent."—Hist. of
Settlement, etc., VII: 409. London, 1783.

[14] Frequent cases occurred to which the following law was applicable: "If
any single woman being a servant by indenture or covenant, have a bastard
child within the time of service, she shall serve such farther time, as beyond
the term of her indenture or covenant mentioned, as the Justice of the
Peace, in the Quarter Sessions, shall think fit as a compensation to her Master or Mistress for the loss and damage they have sustained, by reason of her
bearing such bastard in the time of her servitude; provided it be not more
than two years, nor less than one."—Acts of the Assembly of the Province
of Pennsylvania; p. 27. Phila., 1775.

1726 which failed to receive the recognition of the King, but which came to be recognized as a law in the Province. It provided that no minister should unite in marriage a negro with any white person on penalty of 100 pounds; that any white man or woman living with a negro under pretence of being married should pay a fine of 30 pounds or be sold as a servant not exceeding seven years; that children of such parents be "put out to service" until they arrive at the age of thirty-one years; that if a free negro, man or woman, intermarry with any white man or woman, such negro shall become a slave during life.[15] In Maryland at one period marriages between free born English white women and negro slaves were so frequent that a law was passed in 1663, making the wives of such marriages slaves during the lifetime of their husbands; and the children of such a union were held as slaves for life. Neill in his Terra Mariae, speaks of a domestic of Lord Baltimore who married a negro slave. Through her employer's influence the application of the law was modified in her behalf, but it did not prevent the enslaving of her children.[16]

While penal laws in Pennsylvania empowered masters to bring refractory servants to justice, to lengthen the time of service, to administer corporal punishment, they were no less pronounced, though less in number, in giving servants the right to bring their masters to terms for the abuse of any privilege, or the neglect of any duty. Penn's Frame of Government of 1683, one of the first laws governing the Province, provides "that servants be not kept longer than their time, and such as are careful, be both justly and kindly used in their service, and put in fitting equipage at the expiration thereof according to custom." [17] Even in Maryland where the treatment of servants differed little from that of slaves a law of 1715 provided that any master who "shall deny, and not provide sufficient Meat, Drink, Lodging and Clothing, or shall unreasonably burden servants beyond their strength, with Labor, or debar them of their necessary rest or sleep, or excessively beat and abuse them, or shall give them above ten lashes for any one offence" shall for the first offence be liable to pay a penalty of 1000 pounds of tobacco; and for the third offence the servant shall be set free.[18] In 1665 in the

---

[15] Statutes at Large of Pa. IV: 62—1897.

[16] Ed. D. Neill, Terra Mariae, 203, Phila., 1867.

[17] Section XXIX.

[18] A Compleate Collection of the Laws of Maryland; 1692-1725. Annapolis, 1727.

same province, before the enactment of these laws, one of the court records gives an account of a servant who was brought to trial for running away from his master, "but on account of ill usage and expressing fear of returning, the court set the servant free from his master and mistress." [19] A law of New Jersey provided that in case "any master or mistress be guilty of misusage, refusal of necessary provision, or clothing, or cruelty * * * * to any apprentice or servant" the justice of the peace might set the servant at liberty.[20] In this province, as in Pennsylvania and Maryland, the party aggrieved—either master or servant—had the right of redress, by presenting his complaint to the Justice of the Peace, whose duty it was to judge and punish the offender. This, as it placed the servant in a position that enabled him, without expense, to bring the master to justice, was an important right. In this respect the two were equal before the law, and, while the weaker party, the servant, did not frequently avail himself of the opportunity which the law granted him, the provision was, nevertheless, a considerable barrier against injustice.

---

[19] Maryland Archives; Judicial and Testamentary Business of the Provincial Court, 1649-57. Baltimore, 1891.

[20] Laws of the State of New Jersey, p. 305. New Brunswick, 1800.

CHAPTER X.

THE SERVANT IN THE ARMY.

The enlisting of servants in the royal army at different periods of the history of Pennsylvania was one of the many questions in which the opinion of the Assembly differed from that of the home government. It grew in intensity and bitterness in proportion as the number of servants swelled the ranks of the royal army, and it contributed in no small degree to widen the breach which ultimately led to the separation of the colonies from the mother country. The prominent position which Pennsylvania occupied in the colonial group, with men like Franklin championing the cause of the colony, was significant in adding weight to the opposition of royal authority. Could British recruiting officers enlist servants without the consent of their masters? This was the question upon which the Assembly differed from Parliament. It led at once to the discussion of the legal position of the servant. In the case of slaves, their position was obvious; they were chattels and could no more be taken from the master than his horse or his mule. Owners of servants claimed the same right over their servants whom they had "bought" for a period of years.

The question first arose in Pennsylvania in 1711, when a petition of the free holders stated that "several apprentices and bought servants" had left their masters to enlist in the Queen's service in the province of New Jersey. An act had been passed by the home government to raise money and troops for the war against Canada, and the petitioners complain of "great inequality and hardships falling on such masters as lose servants and yet pay their rates levied upon them for the Queen's use." In this case the grievance was settled to the satisfaction of the masters. It was enacted that every person in the province giving proof to the Lieutenant Governor and Treasurer that servants had enlisted without their consent, should receive ten shillings per month for every servant enlisted, provided, the whole sum did not exceed twenty pounds. Masters who were thus paid, were required to release all claim to the servant, and deliver the indenture to the Governor who could again assign the servant to whom he wished.

Nothing more is heard of the question of enlistment until in 1739, war was declared against Spain, and a demand came from England for supplies and men to form an expedition against the West Indies. Early in the following year, Governor Thomas gave notice in a proclamation in which the recruiting officers were "strictly enjoined not to discover any Person's Name, that shall be desirous to have it concealed." In a postscript he adds, "If any Swedes, Germans, Swissers, or others, will engage a number of their countrymen to enlist in this glorious Expedition, they will receive suitable encouragement in the companies raised by them: The King will supply the troops raised, with arms, clothing and pay, and has engaged his Royal word to send all persons back to their respective habitations when the service shall be over, unless they shall desire to settle themselves elsewhere." [1] This part of the proclamation was intended as a bid for servants, and it had its desired effect. As a result there were numerous complaints of the enlistment of "bought servants" over which the Governor and Assembly wrangled throughout the war period. Nor was it long before the Assembly found an opportunity of retaliating against this proclamation. In answer to a demand for money that body with Franklin as chairman, "resolved, that a warrant do issue to the Treasurer, that he pay the sum of 3000 pounds for the use of our Sovereign George II * * * * provided always, that no warrant do issue from the speaker until all the servants now enlisted in the King's service be returned to their respective masters free of charge, and assurance that no more servants be enlisted or taken from their masters in the future." [2] This grant was made by the Assembly who knew well that the conditions could not be complied with. It would have been impossible to return all servants to their masters had the British officers really desired to do so, and it was therefore a refusal on the part of the assembly to assist in their own defence.

The policy of the Assembly throughout the war was extremely selfish and narrow. They continued to thwart every measure of the Governor and Parliament for the defence of the province, and aid of the Crown, by withholding his salary until he was compelled to yield to their wishes, or resign. The Governor accused them of disloyalty, and of not acting in good faith in their grant of supplies, but they denied this, claiming that they were ready and willing to demonstrate their loyalty and fidelity by giving their due share, on

[1] Pennsylvania Gazette; April 24, 1740.
[2] Colonial Records IV: 459.

7

condition that the "servants so unjustly taken from their masters be returned." Nevertheless, the defiant conclusion of a message to the Governor, June 9th, 1840, shows anything but a willingness to comply with authority, and only increases the bitter feeling between the Governor and the Assembly: "If this be denied the consequences must lie at the Governor's door; and we shall think it our duty on behalf of the great number of freemen of this Province who are injured by the taking and detaining of their servants, to make humble suit to the Crown in their behalf, for that redress we are denied by the Governor."[3] The complaints of the assembly continue. It maintains that a great number of servants are enlisted from the country where labor is difficult to obtain, and where their services are imperatively demanded by the young colony; that the King and Parliament seemed desirous of encouraging the importation of white servants rather than negroes, and if the property of the master is so precarious as to depend upon the will of the servant and the pleasure of an officer, it cannot but be expected that there will be fewer purchasers of servants in the future, and that trade will consequently be much discouraged; that if masters have their property thus taken away, it will not be easy to show that any goods in which they have the most absolute property may not with equal reason be taken from them as their servants.[4]

It appears that the assembly prevailed upon the Governor to order the enlisted servants to be discharged; for a letter from the recruiting officers to the chairman of the assembly, complains that the progress of their companies has been greatly discouraged by the late accounts which have come to them from members of the assembly who gave out that "they do not doubt but all indentured servants enlisted within this province will soon be disbanded; for that assembly, by some proceedings of their house have laid the Governor under necessity of discharging all the servants or apprentices and to oblige those concerned to return them to their respective owners without charge and to the satisfaction of the persons nominated for the purpose."[5] The request of the assembly and Governor, however, was not complied with. The recruiting officers maintained that they had no right to return them to their masters; that they did not know where they lived; that some were called servants who denied being such. They further were of the opinion that discharging

[3] Colonial Records IV: 459.
[4] Ibid. 436-7.
[5] Colonial Records IV: 466.

servants would be dangerous to the public peace; that all subjects not restrained by Parliament, have a right to enlist; that the grievance of the assembly was not so great as had been represented, many having so short a time to serve that the loss to the master would be amply repaid by the detention of the freedom dues; that the number of servants raised could well be spared, and that the loss to the masters could be paid out of the public money.[6]

After a year of controversy between the assembly and the army officers, matters were in the same condition as at the beginning of the war, except that the assembly had persuaded or forced the Governor to make certain concessions. This they accomplished by withholding his salary until he gave way to their demands. In the meantime the army officers were recruiting their ranks from servants as well as freemen, and the assembly, when appealed to, could only reimburse in some measure, the masters for their losses. On the 3d of June, 1741, orders were signed and delivered to James Gibbon and Samuel Lewis, for the payment, by the loan officer of £515-11s-9d, for fifty-eight enlisted servants from Chester County. The next day a petition from the owners of iron works at Coventry and Warwick, stated that ten servants had been taken from them by enlistment; among them were colliers which had put a stop to the works, causing several hundred pounds damage to the petitioners. On July 22nd, an additional sum of £84-11s-11d, was ordered to be paid on account of enlisted servants. Later, Enoch Pearson received £7-10s, and Abraham Emmit £3-13s-7d, each losing one servant by enlistment.[7]

At the breaking out of the French and Indian War, a new and heavier demand was made by the Crown for supplies and men. This again brought up the question of enlistment and revived the conflict between the assembly and royal authority. A law regulating the enlistment was passed by the assembly November 25th, 1755. It contained a provision "that no youth under the age of twenty-one years, nor any bought servant or indentured apprentice shall be admitted to enroll himself or be capable of being enrolled in the companies or regiments without the consent of parents, guardians, or masters, in writing."[8] On the 7th of July in the following

---

[6] Ibid. 468.

[7] History of Chester County (Pa.): 49; Phila., 1881.

[8] Statutes at Large of Pa. V: 200. Phila., 1898. A similar act was passed by the assembly of New Jersey. It was voted that 500 able-bodied freemen or "well affected Indians" be enlisted. To make up this number, criminals

year, it was repealed by the king in council. During the next four years, four similar acts were successively passed by the assembly, and repealed by the crown. While the home government and the assembly were passing laws diametrically opposed to each other, neither party yielding to the other, the army officers issued such orders as they deemed expedient, while the Governor became a sort of a mediator and message bearer between the conflicting parties, favoring at times the assembly, then again the army officers, according as his salary was forthcoming or withheld.

A letter from General Shirley to Colonel Dunbar, September 15th, 1755, shows that in the early part of the war the Colonial authorities avoided as far as possible the enlisting of servants. He writes, "Upon the advices I have received from gentlemen of the greatest zeal for his majesty's service, as well as the best judges in Pennsylvania and other western colonies, I am convinced that the Inlisting of Apprentices and Indentured Servants there, will greatly disserve his interests, as well as be in most cases grievances to the subjects; and would therefore recommend it to you in the strongest manner to avoid doing it." [9] This order seems to have been carefully observed for four months; for the 24th of January in the following year, the president of the council writes to General Shirley as follows: "The officers recruiting here had carefully avoided enlisting indentured servants in obedience to the kind orders of General Braddock in his lifetime, and your Excellency * * * * had given them to that purpose till about three days ago when their Sergeants on beating up for volunteers publicly invited all servants to enlist in his Majesty's service and declared that they had instructions from their superior officers to do so." [10]

The change in General Shirley's instructions marks the beginning of a bitter conflict between that officer and the assembly. Immediately contentions between the masters of servants and the recruiting officers occurred in which, upon this occasion, bloodshed was only avoided by the interposition of some of the magistrates who forbid the enlisting of servants until a further report from General Shirley should arrive. A letter from Governor Morris of February

---

were acquitted and pardoned of all offenses, except felony, committed before the passage of the act, but a penalty of 20 pounds was imposed upon all officers unlawfully enlisting any servants.—Acts of the General Assembly of the Province of N. J. Vol. II: 35.

  [9] Pennsylvania Archives; II: 417; Phila., 1853.

  [10] Colonial Records VI: 777.

12th, 1756, to Sir Charles Hardy, then Governor of New York, admits
the legality of enlisting servants and shows the effect that this practice had at times upon the inhabitants of the colony. He says, "This
is a matter that once before in the administration of Governor
Thomas threw the province into great confusion, and though I have
no doubt concerning the rights of the crown to the personal service
of its subjects in the defence of the Dominions, let their private contract be what they will, yet in the present case I wish the regiments
could have been completed by other means, as it lays a heavy and
very unequal burden upon the inhabitants of this province, and I
am afraid will put my assembly into such a temper as may hinder
them from taking the proper part in the measures concerted for the
common safety." [11]

A day after Governor Morris had sent his letter to Sir Charles
Hardy, he received an address from the assembly into which petitions had in the meantime come from all parts of Pennsylvania, by
masters of servants, complaining of new enlistments. According
to this address, the masters complain that, since they have few
slaves, they are obliged to depend upon servants for tilling the land;
that if servants be at the will of a recruiting officer they will be compelled to use negroes, and the white population will decrease; that
servants must be humored in every way to prevent them from enlisting; that many pretend they will enlist, and when away, do not;
that they are the property of the master by right, especially those
brought to the colony under acts of Parliament, or those becoming
servants under the laws of the colony. [12] This address was immediately sent by the Governor to General Shirley whose reply was
anything but conciliatory. He argues that the king has a right to
the service of indentured servants as well as other volunteers; that
it is now a necessity, that the domain requires it. Against the claim
of illegality he replies that "many instances might be cited to show
that this proposition is not universally true; and as to servants, the
supposition that the king is precluded by contracts between them
and their masters from the rights he had to their service for the defence of his dominions is not founded in the nature of the government in general, and is contrary to the practice of it in the English
constitution." Continuing he says, "When a country is in danger
of being lost to the enemy it is not a time to enter into critical dis-
sertations whether the enlisting of servants many not have a ten-

[11] Pennsylvania Archives, II: 572.
[12] Colonial Records VII: 37.

dency to lessen the importation of them into the country for future tillage of the land, and to increase that of slaves." [13] The only concession which General Shirley made was a promise to order the officers to release such servants as were willing to return to their masters. This, however, was far from satisfying the owners of servants, as but few, if any, had enlisted against their own wishes and consequently remained in the service.

The question of legality was settled by an act of Parliament in 1756. It was enacted that officers in any of his Majesty's forces in America might legally enlist as a soldier, any indentured servant, "any law, custom, or usage to the contrary in any wise not withstanding." To this provision was, however, added, that if the owner of a servant objected within six months after the enlistment, the servant was to be released, or the master was to receive such a sum for the servant as any two justices of the peace should decide. [14]

The proviso of this act which was to give masters a means of redress, seems to have been generally disregarded by the army officers; at any rate servants continued to be enlisted in the royal army against the will of their masters until after the Revolution, and the only means of redress which the owners of servants had, was in the Assembly which frequently passed acts to reimburse such as had lost servants in this manner.

During the Revolution many servants enlisted in the continental forces, and the conflict between the owners of servants, and the military officers, though now transferred entirely to America, still continued. The willingness of this class to enlist in the army in order to escape the service of their masters was sometimes taken advantage of by British officers by offering special inducements to the servant class, including slaves, to leave their masters. When in 1775, Lord Dunmore, Governor of Virginia, after a trifling military success near Norfolk, raised the king's flag and published a proclamation establishing martial law, and requiring every person capable of bearing arms to resort to his standard, under penalty of life and property, he declared freedom "to all indentured servants, negroes, or others appertaining to rebels" if they would "join for the reducing of the colony to a proper sense of its duty." This was a move which Washington considered a great danger to the cause of independence. Referring to Dunmore, he writes, "that man * * * * will be the most formidable enemy of America if some ex-

---

[13] Pennsylvania Archives by S. Hazard, II: 587-92.
[14] Statutes at Large, 29 Geo. II: c. 35, sect. I. Lond., 1764.

pedient cannot be hit upon to convince the servants and slaves of the impotency of his designs." [15]

The Council of Safety in Pennsylvania on the 19th of September, 1776, resolved, that indentured servants and apprentices ought not to be enlisted without the consent of their masters in writing, and that all who have been enlisted should be discharged on application of their masters for that purpose.[16] But these orders like those of the assembly were disregarded by the recruiting officers of the state, and the Supreme Executive Council now attempt to correct what they regard "so distressing to the masters." In 1777 they issue an order "to forbid all recruiting officers in the continental service, and all others, from enlisting servants or apprentices within this state, on pain of being prosecuted with the utmost rigour of the law." [17] The attempts of this body to prevent the enlistment of servants in the army, were, however, like former attempts, at most but a restriction upon a practice which was becoming more common. The numerous claims presented to the state by masters who had lost servants by enlistment, resulted in an act of the assembly, March 12, 1778, which directed the County Treasurers "to pay for servants enlisted into any of the Pennsylvania regiments." To what extent servants enlisted as late as 1781 is shown in a measure from a letter of that year dated February 17th, from the Treasurer of Lancaster county to President Reed. After stating that he had paid £415-10s, by order of the justices to the masters who had lost servants, he says, "I have refused to pay any further order of the Justices on account of Indentured Servants as it will take more money than we will receive in Taxes." [18]

[15] Bancroft, Hist. U. S. VIII: 223, 225. Boston, 1860.
[16] Colonial Records, X: 724.
[17] Col. Rec. Minutes of Sup. EX. Council, XI: 243.
[18] Penn. Arch. S. Hazard, VIII: 730; Phila., 1853.

CHAPTER XI.

THE SOCIAL STATUS OF THE SERVANT.

To give an accurate idea of the social position that the servant of Pennsylvania occupied, is no easy task, because there are almost as many different opinions as there are contemporary accounts. Generalizations, therefore, are meaningless or at best inadequate, especially when applied to a state of society composed of so many diverse elements as were found in that province during the colonial period. There were the Germans, Dutch, English, and Irish, representing different national traits; there were the Quakers and the Presbyterians, believing in different religious creeds. Each of these divisions require a different standard from which to judge of their relation with their fellow men. For example, the Quakers, as a body, took an early stand against the institution of slavery, and it was largely through their influence that Pennsylvania played so prominent a part in the ultimate suppression of the slave trade. A class possessing this spirit of fellow-feeling for all grades of society, naturally regard their servants more on a social equality with themselves, than would the Presbyterians who found a sanction for slavery in the Scriptures.

In a colony like Virginia, composed mainly of English settlers, with common political and religious ideas, the treatment, and social condition of the servant may be estimated in a more general way; but in Pennsylvania where nearly every county was made up of a population differing in nationality and religious beliefs from those about it, no such estimate can be regarded as adequate. Society was factional, disunited; a belief or an opinion held by one faction was a sufficient ground for an adverse opinion by the other. The Quakers regarded the Presbyterians as the same as the Massachusetts Puritans who had whipped their co-religionists and put four of them to death, and they were quite determined on squaring the account. So bitter was the hatred betwen the Scotch-Irish and the Germans that the former on one occasion had a full intention of attacking the latter and marched with that intention armed to Germantown, the stronghold of their enemies. On this occasion, however, the Quakers broke with their traditional peace policy and armed themselves against their aggressors. The Palatines, driven from the Rhine by war and famine, were naturally prompted by different motives than were the shiftless vagrants coming from the cities of England. It was to a large extent upon this difference of nationality, character, or religious belief, that the behavior of a servant, or the conduct of a master depended.

In any system of servitude the master by virtue of his position possesses advantages over the servant. He may be domineering or abusive in such a way as to make it difficult for those subordinate to him to find redress; equal rights before the law by no means implies social equality, and sometimes not legal equality in fact. While there were laws granting to servants the right to bring their masters to justice, for any cruel or unjust treatment, there seems to have been few occasions upon which this right was exercised. In the year 1700, the Governor and Council of Maryland received a complaint from a certain inhabitant, stating that a servant of his, a schoolmaster, whom he had corrected, had applied to a magistrate for a peace warrant against him. The Council considering the matter decided not to countenance the servant, "for it was not customary to allow servants to swear the peace against their masters, and it might be very inconvenient." [1] The same in practice was true in Pennsylvania, and in fact in all colonies that had servants. There is little evidence to show that servants applied to magistrates for protection. Their method of redress, when ill treated, was usually found in running away, and if taken up and brought before the court, they would plead cruel treatment as the cause of leaving, and if their complaint was well founded, they would sometimes get their freedom.

A law of 1700 provided that no servant could be compelled to work on Sunday. A fine of twenty shillings was imposed for every violation of this act, and though it was repealed six years later, it became a general rule in Pennsylvania, and seems to have been a customary practice in all of the colonies. George Alsop, in his "Character of the Province of Maryland," represents the condition of servants as being very mild: "Five days and a half in the summer weeks is the allotted time that they work in; and for two months when the sun predominates in the highest pitch of his heat, they claim an ancient and customary privilege, to repose themselves three hours a day within the house, and this is undeniably granted to them

---

[1] J. R. Brackett, The Negro in Maryland, p. 24. Baltimore, 1889.

that work in the field." But it must be remembered that Alsop writes to encourage immigration into Maryland, and naturally represents conditions in as favorable a light as possible. A better authority, though representing the opposite extreme is William Eddis, an English traveler in America, and eight years a resident, who writes in 1770. He declares "they are strained to the utmost to perform their allotted labor; and, from a prepossession in many cases too justly founded, they are supposed to be receiving the just reward which is due to repeated offences. There are doubtless many exceptions to this observation, yet, generally speaking, they groan beneath a worse than Egyptian bondage,"[2] Eddis condemns the system of indentured service from start to finish. The inhabitants of Maryland, he writes, treat the convicts the same as indentured servants, and not unfrequently show them more consideration, regarding them more profitable, as their term is for seven years, while that of indentured servants is only five. "Negroes bound for life are nearly always more comfortable than the Europeans over whom the rigid planter exercises an inflexible severity." The situation of the free willers, he observes, is, in almost every instance more to be lamented than either that of the convict or the indentured servant; further, that the inhabitants of Maryland doubted whether people with unimpeachable character would come to America to accept a servile position; that character is of little value, and little regarded by masters in search of laborers; that they were not often disposed to hire such as expected to be gratified in full proportion to their acknowledged qualifications. "From this detail," he concludes, "I am persuaded, you will no longer imagine, that servants in this country, are in a better situation than those in Great Britain."[3] Although Eddis' description represents an extreme condition, it must nevertheless be regarded as a correct picture of a large class of the servants in Maryland. Even convicts sometimes chose severe penalties in preference to a term of servitude.

In Pennsylvania their condition was somewhat better than in Maryland, and yet their condition here was often little better than that of slaves.[4] Mittleberger, whose authority seems trustworthy, says, "Our Europeans who are purchased must always work hard, for new fields are constantly laid out. * * * * However hard

---

[2] Letters from America: 70.
[3] William Eddis, Letters from America: 69-75.
[4] History of Westmoreland County: 59. Phila., 1882.

one may be compelled to work in his Fatherland, he will surely find it quite as hard, if not harder, in the new country." [5]

The number of convicts in the colonies did much to bring the entire servant class into disrepute. The blending of this vicious element with the rest of the population gave the laboring class, and especially the servants who were too often regarded on the same plane with convicts, a deteriorating tendency which affected the whole state of society. Franklin, in the Gazette, makes frequent mention of the criminals and their pernicious influence on the public morals. [6]

In spite of the many contemporary accounts, favorable to the character of the servant class,—and there were many examples of honesty and integrity among them,—there is much evidence to lead one to believe that a large proportion lived upon a low moral plane. In a pamphlet written in verse, entitled the "Sot-Weed-Factor, or a Voyage to Maryland," [7] a great deal of light is thrown on the state of society as it existed in the colonies about 1700, and especially on the character of women servants. The moral tone was low. Illiteracy prevailed among all classes. The factor mentions "A reverend Judge, who to the shame of all the bench could write his name," and adds by way of explanation, that "in the county court of Maryland, very few of the justices of the peace can read or write." On one occasion the factor was entertained at the home of a planter who owned a number of female servants. By one who he says "passed for a chambermaid," he was conveyed to his room. Her degraded appearance led him to make inquiries concerning her past; when she, with an affected blush, replied:

> "In better times e'er to this Land
> I was unhappily trapann'd;
> Perchance as well I did appear,
> As any Lord or Lady here.

---

[5] Journey to Pennsylvania: 30.

[6] A writer who styles himself "America," in the Gazette of May 9, 1751, commenting sarcastically on "that good and wise act of Parliament by virtue of which all the Newgates and Dungeons in Great Britain are emptied into the Colonies," says, "Our Mother knows what is best for us. What is a little House-breaking, Shop-lifting, or Highway-robbing; what is a son now and then corrupted and hanged, a Daughter debauched, and Pox'd, a wife stabbed, a Husband's throat cut, or a child's brains beat out with an Axe, compared with this 'Improvement and Well peopling of the Colonies.'"

[7] Written by a certain Ebenezer Cook; London, 1807. The "Sot-Weed-Factor" was a tobacco agent.

> Not then a slave for twice two Year.
> My Cloaths were fashionably new,
> Nor were my shifts of Linnen Blue;
> But things are changed, now at the Hoe,
> I daily work and Barefoot go,
> In weeding Corn or feeding Swine,
> I spend my melancholy Time." *

In justice to Pennsylvania it must be remembered that the above quotation applies to Maryland; however, the social life in Pennsylvania, in the middle of the 18th century, according to Mittleberger, is very much like that described by the Sot-Weed-Factor. "If any one," he says, "has lost a wife or a husband in Germany, * * * * he or she can find such lost treasure, if the same be still alive, in America, for Pennsylvania is the gathering place of all runaways and good-for-nothings." *

Samuel Breck, whose trustworthiness is not questioned, and whose observation of the system covered a period of many years, gives valuable information concerning the servant class in Pennsylvania at the beginning of the present century. In his Note Book, dated December 22, 1807, he writes, "The vast quantity of unculti-

---

* "Kidnapp'd and fool'd I hither fled,
  To shun a hated Nuptial bed,
  And to my cost already find,
  Worse Plagues than those I left behind."

To avoid an unhappy marriage, is the general excuse made by English women who are sold or sell themselves to Maryland.

On another occasion the factor, while stopping at an inn, describes a "jolly female crew" that "were deep engaged in Lanctre-Looe (cards):"

> "In Night rails white, with dirty mien,
> Such sights are scarce in England seen:
> I thought them first some Witches bent,
> On black Designs in dire Convent,
> Till one who with affected air,
> Had nicely learned to curse and swear;
> D—n you, says one, though now so brave
> I knew you late a Four-Years Slave;
> What if for Planter's wife you go,
> Nature designed you for the Hoe.
> Rot you, replies the other straight,
> The Captain kissed you for his Freight;
> And if the Truth was known aright,
> And how you walked the Streets at Night,
> You'd blush (if one cou'd blush) for shame,
> Who from Bridewell or Newgate came."

* Journey to Pennsylvania: 92.

vated land, the general prosperity and unexampled increase of our cities, unite to scatter the menial citizens, and to make it extremely difficult to be suited with decent servants. I have had a strange variety, amongst which I have heard of one being hung, of one that hung himself, of one that died drunk in the road, and of another that swallowed poison in a fit of intoxication. Those that form my present household, have lived with me from one to three years, and are pretty tolerable." Again under date of August 1, 1817, we find the following: "Being a long time dissatisfied with some of my servants, I went on board the ship John, from Amsterdam, lately arrived with four hundred passengers, to see if I could find one for Mrs. Ross and two for myself. I saw the remains of a very fine cargo, consisting of healthy, good looking men, women and children, and I purchased one German Swiss for Mrs. Ross, and two French Swiss for myself." Three years later he writes of a servant girl who was discharged "for fibbing and mischief-making." Commenting further upon the same servant, he says. "But what makes me take any notice of this woman is that she, like many others who have served in my house these last twenty-five years, came to us almost naked, and must have seen hard times without profiting by the lessons of adversity; for no sooner was she entitled to receive a few dollars, than she squandered them in finery instead of buying necessaries." After describing the thoughtless extravagance in which his servants lavished money in the purchase of jewelry and other "trash," he adds, "This is a faithful picture of the wasteful and disgraceful extravagance of nine-tenths of the servants, male and female, for the last thirty years.[10]

Servants from the continent were usually preferred to those from England and Ireland. "The Irish servants," writes Benjamin Marshall in 1766, "will be very dull, such numbers having already arrived from different ports, that I believe it will be overdone, especially as several Dutch vessels are expected here, which will always command the market."[11] Those from England seem often to have been "picked up from the streets of London," and to have come from the cities generally, whereas those from Germany were usually from the country and, therefore, better suited to develop the agricultural resources of the colony.

Perhaps in nothing was the influence of the servant more marked

[10] Samuel Breck, Recollections, etc. p. 295-300. Phila., 1877.
[11] Letter Book of Benjamin Marshall, in Pa. Mag. of Hist. and Biog. XX: 212. Phila., 1896.

in his effect on society, than in that powerful agency for good or evil—the public school system. In some of the colonies it was largely the redemptioners and indentured servants that instructed the youths of the time. Nor was the average schoolmaster of those days a model of excellence. In fact he was not supposed to be, and his character was usually in keeping with his reputation. Too often their moral standard was low, their habits dissolute, and their methods and discipline extremely crude. That sobriety was at a premium among this class may be inferred from the following advertisement: "Wanted, a sober person that is capable of teaching a school; such a one coming well recommended, may find encouragement in said employ." [12] It has been stated that in the early part of the 18th century, three-fourths the instruction received in Maryland was derived from instructors that were either indentured servants or transported felons. There is no evidence that convicts were thus employed in Pennsylvania, but the servant formed no small proportion of the teaching force of the community. Scarcely a vessel arrived in which there were not schoolmasters regularly advertised for sale. What the effect of such instruction on a growing colony must have been, is obvious. The fact that the free population intrusted the instruction of their children to these crude moulders of youthful thought does not indicate an advanced state of society in general, and yet it must be remembered that those were pioneer days in which the question of subsistence was necessarily uppermost in the mind of the individual. In none of the middle colonies at this time did the teacher occupy an exalted position. He was regarded as an unproductive laborer. Agricultural laborers or artisans was what the colony wanted and most needed, and they were nearly always sold at a higher price than the schoolmasters.

It would, however, be incorrect to regard what has been said, as a just representation of the entire servant class. Against the unfavorable accounts given by some contemporaries, may be placed others representing the highest types of honesty, industry, and nobility. Robert Sutcliff, who visited America, at the beginning of the present century, writes, "I noticed many families, particularly in Pennsylvania, of great respectability both in our society and

[12] Pennsylvania Gazette; Dec. 11, 1755.

"Wanted, a single Person, well qualified for a Schoolmaster. Such a one coming well recommended, may meet with encouragement by applying to John Braughton, within a few miles of Rariton Landing."—Ibid; Aug. 18, 1755.

amongst others, who had themselves come over to this country as redemptioners; or were children of such. And it is remarkable, that the German residents in this country, have a character for greater industry and stability than those of any other nation." [18] A large proportion of the Germans in Pennsylvania, whose thrift and industry Sutcliff commends, we have already seen, were servants. The same writer speaks of a German who "being of the class of immigrants called redemptioners" came to Pennsylvania, and was first employed as a waiting boy. After he learned the English language he requested of his master to be put apprentice to a paper maker, which request was granted. Having acquired a knowledge of the manufacture of paper, by industry and economy he obtained sufficient property to enable him to begin business, and in a short time he was the owner of a large manufacturing concern. Examples of this kind might be multiplied, showing that many of this servile class, after being released from the indenture, became distinguished citizens. No less a person than Charles Thompson, Secretary of Congress during the Revolution, was said to have been a redemptioner. It was this class that contributed a signer to the immortal Declaration of Independence in the person of Mathew Thornton. It was this species of servitude that gave to the war for independence the efficient General Sullivan, who shared the glory of having fought with Washington.

After the servant had completed his period of service, he was entitled to a legal settlement. This was fixed by an act of the Assembly of Pennsylvania in 1771, providing that "every indentured servant, legally and directly imported into this province shall obtain a legal settlement * * * * in the place in which such servant shall first serve * * * * the space of sixty days." If during his indenture he had been sold to another master, and served with him twelve months, he obtained a legal settlement in the place where he last served. [14] Thus the servant was merged into the great body of freemen, and all traces of his former occupations were soon obliterated. If he were industrious, he could rise, as in fact many did, to the highest social and political plane, by virtue of those qualities which elevated all freemen to positions of trust and influence. As a matter of fact, however, the servants on becoming free, swelled the ranks of the great middle class, and the prominent positions which many occupied in after life, were, after all, relatively few.

---

[18] Sutcliff, Travels in America: 257. London, 1811.

[14] Laws of the Commonwealth of Pennsylvania, I: 577. Phila., 1797.

CONCLUSION.

What, finally, was the result of the system of indentured service on the society and the state? This may be said: It was an institution arising out of the economic conditions of the time, suited to, and justified by the state of society. Just as the feudal system of Europe was a necessary step in the evolution of society from a lower to a higher form of civilization, so the institution of indentured service was a necessary stage in the economic development of the colonial society of Pennsylvania. It had a definite purpose, was called into existence by natural forces, served that purpose, and then with the increase of labor and the invention of machinery, gradually passed away. That it was economically superior to a system of free labor under colonial conditions, is apparent from the fact that it was everywhere preferred to the system of hired service. The benefit to production from long and certain terms of contract labor in a sparsely settled country no doubt outweighed the incidental though necessary evils. The moral effect on society was deteriorating, as any species of servitude must necessarily be. It hardened the master toward the servile class and prepared him for slavery.[1] And yet, indirectly, there was a moral advantage to the state as a whole; the system served as a barrier against the growing institution of slavery for which it was substituted, thus preventing the moral degradation which that institution carried with it. The public attention which this institution called to transportation, resulted in better laws governing immigration in general. The authorities, by reason of the legal processes necessary in landing and binding servants, were forced to take measures to correct abuses which otherwise would have escaped their notice. The infusion of the lower and middle classes into society was marked by an increase of democratic ideas which gave to Pennsylvania society that peculiar and unique cast which typically foreshadowed the future commonwealths of America. It stimulated immigration, bringing into Pennsylvania both a desirable and an unworthy class. Those who came with the high motives of building up the colony by establishing permanent homes, who were driven from their native countries by wars and famine, and by religious and political persecutions, were a decided advantage to society and the state. Chief among

---

[1] J. C. Ballagh, Johns Hopkins Univ. Hist. Series, Vol. XIII.

this class were the German Palatines. These from the earliest days had been disciplined in the habits of industry, frugality and patience, and were peculiarly fitted for the laborious occupations of felling timber, clearing lands, and forming the first improvements. The success which attended their efforts induced thousands of their enterprising countrymen to abandon their homes, secure passage and sell themselves as servants in Pennsylvania, there to develop the uncultivated wastes into a prosperous state. Nor because they came in the humble capacity of servants were the hardy, brave, though hot-headed Scotch-Irish, who hated the Pope "as sincerely as they venerated Calvin or Knox" an unimportant element in developing the resources of the new colony and infusing a sturdy strength into the future state. Likewise the conservative and resolute English who came with the first settlers as servants, and who throughout the colonial period continued to arrive in servile capacity, introducing trade, manufacture and arts, were of inestimable value. Their genius supplemented the work of the other classes, preserved English institutions and customs, and advanced the educational interests which placed the state in its prominent rank at the close of the Revolution.

But alongside the honest and industrious which the system of indentured service was instrumental in bringing to the colony, came the shiftless, the idle, the vagrant, the pauper, and finally the convict, who too often received the same consideration as the honest servant. This class naturally cast a shadow over the whole body of indentured service, and their influence was decidedly bad. It is not strange that a writer in Franklin's Gazette of 1751 thought that "all the Newgates and Dungeons in Britain" were emptied into the colonies, or that "these Thieves and Villains introduced among us, spoil the Morals of the Youths and the Neighborhoods that entertain them," for the number of this class that came into the colony in the guise of servants and redemptioners gave justification to the statement. Their effect on the social and moral life of the colony could not have been other than detrimental.

But perhaps the worst results of the system were connected with transportation. Shipping merchants were not slow to see the profits arising from the sale of servants far above the actual cost of transportation. Various agencies were employed to secure passengers. Vessels were crowded beyond their capacity so that the death rate became enormous. The Neulanders, the "spirits," the "soul-drivers," were busily employed in practices of deception, and artful

8

misrepresentations which caused many immigrants to spend a disappointed life in the new colony. All this, aside from the human suffering and injustice inflicted upon thousands, involved an economic loss.

A final estimate of the result of the system of indentured service cannot be adequate without a definite statement of the point of view from which the system is to be judged; and no single criterion can be adopted from which to estimate the complete results in all its relations. To Germany this vast emigration meant a loss of her best population; to England it was an advantage, as it offered a partial solution to the problem of "What to do with the idle classes?" and to Pennsylvania it meant a decided economic gain. Like slavery it performed the menial labor of the community in which it existed, but unlike that institution when public sentiment demanded its extinction it died, by virtue of the limited term of service, an easy and natural death, almost unnoticed by those living in that period; no clash of arms nor shedding of human blood marked its extinction; and although to-day in almost every community in the United States may be found those who remember vividly the stories related by parents and relatives of the suffering caused, in part at least, by this system of service, there is no trace of its former disfigurement left upon the great Commonwealth of Pennsylvania.

APPENDIX I.

Form for binding a servant.

Philadelphia, **ss.**

This Indenture Witnesseth That Peter Smith of his own free will (and consent of his Father, John Smith) for and in consideration as well of the Sum of $100 paid by Edwin Valette of the N. L. of the City of Philadelphia, Ship Brohen, to Jacob Sperry, for his passage from Amsterdam, as also for other causes and considerations he the said Peter Smith Hath bound and put himself, and by these Presents Doth bind and put himself Servant to the sd Edwin Vallette to Serve him his Executors Administrators and Assigns from the day of the date hereof for and during the full term of Three years from thence next ensuing—During all which said term the said Servant his Said Masters his Executors Administrators and Assigns faithfully Shall serve, and that honestly and obediently in All things, as a good and faithful servant ought to do. And the said Edwin Vallette his Executors Administrators and Assigns during the said term shall find and provide for the sd Servant sufficient Meat Drink Apparel Washing and Lodging—and also to give him 18 weeks' Schooling—And at the expiration of his term the said Servant to have two complete Suits of Clothes, one whereof to be new—And for the true performance the Covenants and Agreements aforesaid the Said Parties bind themselves unto each other firmly by these Presents. In Witness Whereof the Said Parties have interchangeably set their Hands and Seals hereunto. Dated the — day of —— in the Year of our Lord one Thousand eight hundred and ——.
Bound before ————

I. F. H., Register.

PETER SMITH,   (Seal).
JOHN SMITH,   (Seal).
E. VALLETTE,   (Seal).

Copied from MSS. Registry of the Redemptioners in Hist. Soc. of Pa.

APPENDIX II.

Form for transferring a servant from one owner to another.

Philadelphia, ss.

I the within named Edwin Vallette, in consideration of the Sum of $75 to me in hand paid by Daniel K. Miller of the N. L. of the

9

City of Philadelphia, Potter, the receipt whereof I do hereby acknowledge. Have and by these Presents Do assign transfer and Set
over unto the sd D. K. M. his Executor, Administrator and Assigns
the within Indenture and all my Right Interest Claim and demand
whatsoever of in and to the same and to the service of the within
named Servant Peter Smith therein agreed to be performed for and
during the remainder of the Term of the within Indenture yet to
come and unexpired—He the sd D. K. M. his Ex'rs Adm'rs, and
Assigns performing the Covenants and Agreements in the within
Indenture contained which on the part of the sd E. V. his Ex. Ad.
and As. are and ought to be paid and performed as within mentioned—Witnesseth my Hand and Seal this —— day of ————
in the Year of our Lord one Thousand Eight hundred and ————.
Before

    I. F. H., ·   E. VALLETTE.
     ·Register.

From MSS. in Hist. Soc'y of Penn.

APPENDIX III.

Following are a number of entries as they appear in the Registry
of Redemptioners, now in the Historical Society of Pennsylvania
library. Two manuscript volumes contain the names of all the
German redemptioners bound at Philadelphia from 1784 to 1831.

Dec. 15,   John Hesselbach and Anna Elizabetha his wife bound
1784.   themselves Servants to Frederick Boulange of the city
            of Philadelphia, Merchant, to Serve him four years, to
            have customary Freedom Suits.

                                 Consideration 40 pounds.

Sept. 10,   Johannes Hesselback and Anna Elizabetha his wife·
1788.   bound themselves Servants to John Edwards of Thorn-
            burry Township, Chester County, State of Pennsylvania,
            Iron Master, to Serve him four years, to have Customary
            freedom Suits, their first Indenture recorded page 69,
            being cancelled by their own request.

                                 Consideration 30 Pounds.·

Oct. 19,   George Roth and his wife Anna Guster and their child
1795.   Anna Maria Bound to Charles Gregwere, of Philadel-
            phia County, Dublin Township, Farmer, to serve him
            three years each and Twenty Dollars the husband to

have besides the freedom dues, one new pair of Boots, their child Anna Maria to have Freedom suits, to be furnished books to learn in & to be free when the Parents are.   Consideration L57-84-

Aug. 22, 1800.   John Andrew Maurer his wife Anna Barbary, Son John Andrew and Daughters Anna Barbara and Catherine Elizabeth, have bound themselves to Samuel Ringgold Esq'r in the State of Maryland, to serve him Four years, the son to have two quarters' schooling, and each of them to have customary Freedom Suits.
                                           Consideration 100 Guineas.

Nov. 5, 1817.   Elizabeth Seiffer bound herself servant to William Hayes of Lewisbury, Union County, Merch' to serve him for Two years and Six months. And at the expiration of her term to have two complete suits of Clothes, one thereof to be new, and Ten Dollars in cash.
                                           Cons' 70 Doll's.

Nov. 5, 1817.   Catharina Sterki with her Father's consent bound herself servant to Richard Ashurst of Philad'a Merch.' to serve him Three years. And to have Six weeks' of schooling for every year of her servitude, and at the Expiration of her term to have Two Complete suits of Clothes, one thereof to be new.
                                           Cons'n. 66 30-100 Doll's.

Nov. 5, 1817.   Hans Ulrich Kaser with his Father's consent bound himself servant to Jacob Hassinger of Philad'a Merch' to serve him 8 years and 3 months, and to have 6 weeks' schooling for every year of his servitude, and at the Expiration of his term to have two complete Suits of Clothes, one thereof to be new.
                                           Cons'n 66 30-100 Doll's.

Nov. 5, 1817.   Catharine Klinger bound herself servant to John Gest of Philad'a Merch't, to serve him Four years and at the Expiration of her term to have Two Complete suits of clothes one thereof to be new.   Cons'n 100 Doll's.
Catharine Klinger at the same time assigned to Frederick Diller Baker of Sallsburry township Lancaster County, Farmer to serve him the remainder of her Indenture as above recorded.   Cons'n 100 Doll's.

Nov. 10,-- Landelin Stregel with his wife's consent bound himself
servant to Parkes Boyd to serve him Three years, And to
have Fifteen Dollars per year in lieu of Apparel and no
Freedom suit.   Cons'n 15 Doll's.

Nov. 10,   Anna Maria Stregel with her husband's consent bound
1817.   herself servant to the above Parkes Boyd to serve him
Three years and to have Fifteen Dollars per year in lieu
of Apparel and no Freedom suit.   Cons'n 15 Doll's.

Jan.   1, Landelin Stregel Assigned by Parkes Boyd to Christian
1818.   G. Schmidt of Philad'a Baker to serve him the remainder of his Indenture as recorded page 5.
                                     Cons'n 20 Doll's.

Jan.   1, Anna Maria Stregel assigned by Parkes Boyd to the
1818. ·   above Christian G. Schmidt to serve him the remainder
of her Indenture as recorded, page 5.
                                     Cons'n 20 Doll's.

Jan.   1, John Andrew Schneider bound himself servant to John
1818.   Geisinger of Hanover township Northampton County
Farmer to serve him Three years. And at the Expiration of his term to have two complete suits of Clothes,
One thereof to be new, And fifteen Dollars in Cash.
                                 Cons'n 16 30-100 Doll.

Oct. 22,   Anna Maria Ott with consent of her husband ————
1818.   to James Fassitt of Philad'a Merch't for Two years to
have at the end of the Term Two Complete Suits of
Clothes, one thereof to be new. And should the Servant .
during the term of her Servitude have an Offspring then
she is to serve her Master Six Months' longer.
                                     Cons'n 55 Dol's.

Nov. 30,   Anna Maria Ott assigned by William Warrance, to John
1819.   Kohler of Phila. Coach wheel wright, to serve him or
assigns the remainder of her Indenture recorded Page
76.   Cons'n 20 Dol's.

Nov. 30,   Christian Ott and his wife Anna Maria, having paid the
1819.   above John Kohler Thirty Six dol's in consideration of
the remainder of their Indentures, they are both discharged from any further Obligations contained therein
and the Indentures made null and void.

Jan. 22, Eva Wagner with consent of her father to John M.
1821. Brown of the Northern Libertyes, Phila. County, Riger,
for five years, to have six months' schooling and at the
end of the term Two complete suits of clothes, one of
which to be new, also one Straw bed, one bedstead, one
Blanket, one pillow and one sheet. Con'n 70 Dol's.

Jacob Schaeffer, with his own consent assigned by Jacob
Sheerer to Frederick Snyder of the city of Philadelphia,
Baker, to serve the remainder of the term of his Inden-
ture, Recorded page 129. Con. $24.

APPENDIX IV.

Health Officer's Certificate permitting Passenger to land.

Health Office, Phila.,

March 10, 1824.

To I. F. H. Register of German Passengers,

I do hereby report that I have reviewed all the above named
passengers (25 in number) on board the ship Iane, Capt. John
Smith, arrived this day at the Port of Phila. from Amsterdam, and
that none of them are superannuated, impotent or otherwise likely
to become chargeable to the Public, but all of them sound, without
any defect in mind or body.

WM. MANDRY,

Health Officer.

Copied from the Registry of Redemptioners, MSS.

APPENDIX V.

Notices of Runaways.

"Runaway last Night, from on board the Dianna, of Dublin,
Richard M"Carty, Master, a Servant Man, named Valentine Hand-
lin, aged about 30 Years, a lusty rawbon'd Fellow small round
Visaged, is of a dark Complexion with short Black Hair, Had on
when he went away, a brown bob Wig, Old Felt Hat, an old lightish
colour'd cloth grear Coat, a blue grey Waistcoat, old leather
Breeches, yarn Stockings, broad square toe'd Shoes; and perhaps
may have taken some other clothes with him. He is remarkably

hollow Footed and seems crump footed when his Shoes are off. Whoever secures the said Servant so he may be had again, shall have Twenty Shillings Reward, paid by

WILLIAM BLAIR."

Pennsylvania Gazette, Dec. 11, 1740.

"Run away from Cornwall iron works, in Lancaster County, an English Servant Man, named Mathew Williams, belonging to William Keepers, of Baltimore County, in Maryland, a short well set fellow, about 25 years of age: Had on when he went away a castor hat, silk cap, a blue broad-cloth coat, and black damask Jacket, red plush breeches and a pair of boots. Whoever takes up the said servant and brings him to Amos Garrett, at said works shall receive 5 Pounds as a reward paid by

AMOS GARRETT."

Pennsylvania Gazette, May 16, 1751.

"Run away from Henry Caldwell, of Newton, in Chester County, an Irish Servant-man, named John Hamilton, about 22 years of age, of a middle stature, well set, fresh complexion, and speaks good English: Had on when he went away, a brown colour'd coat, white damask vest, very much broke, old felt hat, cotton cap, good leather breeches, Light coloured stockings, and old shoes; he has been a servant before, and is supposed to have his old indenture with him.

Whoever takes up said servant, so that his master may have him again, shall have 30s. reward, and reasonable charges paid by

HENRY CALDWELL."

Pennsylvania Gazette, March 17, 1752.

"Run away on the 18th inst. at night from on board the ship Friendship, Hugh Wright, Commander, now lying at William Allen Esquire's wharff, James Dowdall, a servant man, a laborer, lately come in, but has been in many parts of this continent before; he is about 5 ft. 4 inches high, has short hair, but neither cap nor hat: Has on a blue frize coat and Jacket, a Check shirt, leather breeches, and blue yarn hose: speaks as a native of this Province; he is at present greatly infected with the itch, and not able to travel far. Whoever secures the said James Dowdall so that he be brought to the said Commander, or to Wallace and Bryan on Market Street Wharf, shall have 40s. reward and reasonable charges paid by

WALLACE AND BRYAN."

Pennsylvania Gazette, Sept. 28, 1752.

"Run away the 20 ult. from Philip Moser: A Servant Man named Nicholas Wolfe five feet five inches high, having lost the little finger of his left hand, black hair'd; had on when he went away, a light grey cloth coat, blue Jacket new shoes with yellow buckles in them. Whoever takes up and secures him so that his master may have him again, shall have *Five Pounds* and all reasonable charges paid by

PHILIP MOSER."

Pa. Journal and Weekly Advertiser, Jan. 26, 1763.

A COURT RECORD OF A RUNAWAY.

"Abell Porter, plt

An action of the case.

Henry Bowman

The plt declares that his Servant Henry Williams, a Cooper being run away and taken up in those parts the de'ft. did engage and promise to be security for his forth coming upon demand, and the deft. now refusing to procure or produce the said servant, the pl't. craves judgment of this court against the deft. for the sum of thirty-five pounds ster: money of old England with costs; The def't doth own in open court that he did promise to be security for the sd servant's forth coming according to declaration but craves a Refferance till next court which the court granted."

Ancient Records of Sussex Co. (Pa.) MSS. 1681-1709.

APPENDIX VI.

Warrant of Survey of "Servant-land."

"At the Request of John Baldwin that we would grant him to take up One hundred acres of head-land at One-half penny Rent per acre per annum, fifty thereof in right of his own service to Joshua Hastings and fifty in right of his Wife Katharine, servant to John Blunston. These are to authorize and Require thee to survey and lay out to the said John Baldwin the said number of One hundred acres of land in the tract appropriated to servants or elsewhere in the province not already surveyed nor taken up, etc." Dated 30th 4 mo., 1702.

Quoted in History of Chester Co., Phila., 1881. P. 155.

BIBLIOGRAPHY.

Acts of the Assembly of the Province of Pennsylvania. Philadelphia, 1775.

Acts of the General Assembly of the Province of New Jersey, by Samuel Nevill, ii. Woodbridge, N. J., 1761.

Acts of the General Assembly of the Commonwealth of Pennsylvania, 1819-'20. Harrisburg, 1820.

Acts of the Parliament of Scotland, etc., vi, part ii. 1772.

Acts of the Parliament of Scotland, x. 1823.

Acts of the General Assembly of the Province of Pennsylvania, 1817-18. Harrisburg, 1818.

Alsop, George, A Character of the Province of Maryland; printed from London ed. of 1666, in Maryland Historical Society. Baltimore, 1880.

American Colonial Tracts, Monthly, No. 3-July, 1897, Vol. i; pub. by Geo. P. Humphrey. Rochester, 1897-8.

Ancient Records of Sussex County (Pa.), 1681-1709. Historical Society of Pennsylvania Library.

Ballagh, J. C., White Servitude in the Colony of Virginia; Johns Hopkins University series, Vol. 13. Baltimore, 1895.

Bancroft, George, History of the United States. Boston, 1874.

Bettle, Edward, Notices of negro Slavery as Connected with Pennsylvania; Mem. of Hist. Soc. of Pa., i. Philadelphia, 1864.

Board of Trade Journals, transcripts in Hist. Soc. Penn. Vols. iv and x.

Brackett, J. R., The Negro in Maryland. Baltimore, 1889.

Breck, Samuel, Recollections; edited by H. E. Scudder. Philadelphia, 1877.

Brissot, J. P., New Travels in the United States of America. London, 1794.

Bruce, P. A., Economic History of Virginia. London, N. Y., 1896.

Byrd, W., Slavery and Indentured Servants, in Am. Hist. Rev. Vol. i.

Calendar of State Papers, Colonial; ed. by W. N. Sainsbury. London, 1860.

Calendar of State Papers, Colonial; America and West Indies; 1661 to 1676. London, 1880-93.

Century Magazine, (E. Eggleston), 46:625.

Chalmers, George, Political Annals of the Present United colonies from their settlement to the Peace of 1763. London, 1780.

Charters and Acts of the Assembly of the Province of Pennsylvania. Philadelphia, 1762.

Cobb, S. H., The Story of the Palatines. New York, 1897.

Collection of all the Laws of the Province of Pennsylvania. Philadelphia, 1742.

Collection of New Jersey Historical Society; Vol. i. Newark, 1874.

Colonial Records (of Pa.) esp. vols. ii, iii, and iv.

Complete Collection of the Laws of Maryland; 1692-1725. Annapolis, 1727.

Continental Sketches of Distinguished Pennsylvanians, D. R. B. Nevin. Philadelphia, 1875.

Cook, Ebenezer, The Sot-Weed-Factor, or A Voyage to Maryland. London, 1708.

Court Papers of Philadelphia County; MSS. in Historical Society of Pennsylvania Library.

DeFoe, Daniel, Colonel Jack; Moll Flanders.

Documents Relating to the Colonial History of New York, vol. v. Albany, 1855.

Doyle, J. A., English Colonies in America; vol. ii. New York, 1882.

Du Bois, W. E. B., The Suppression of the African Slave Trade. New York, 1896.

Duke of Yorke's Book of Laws.

Eddis, William, Letters from America, Historical and Descriptive, 1769-77. London, 1792.

Evangelical Review, (R. Weiser), 21 :290.

Fearon, Henry B., Sketches of America. London, 1819.

Fisher, G. S., Making of Pennsylvania. Philadelphia, 1896.

Fiske, John, The Dutch and Quaker Colonies in America. Boston and New York, 1899.

Force, Peter, Tracts and other Papers of the Colonies in North America, vol. ii. Washington, 1844.

Franklin, Benjamin, Works, ed. by J. Bigelow. New York, 1888.

Georgia Historical Collection, (A Voyage to Georgia), vols. i and ii. Savannah, 1840.

Gordon, Thomas, The History of Pennsylvania. Philadelphia, 1829.

Grahame, James, The History of the United States of America. 1845.

Grants, Concessions and Original Constitutions of New Jersey. Philadelphia, 1752.

Hallesche Nachrichten, Neue Aufgabe I; reprinted at Allentown (Pa.), 1886.

Halle Reports, vol. i, by W. J. Mann. Reading (Pa.), 1882.

Hart, A. B., American History Told by Contemporaries, i, 1492-1689. New York, 1897.

Hazard, Samuel, Annals of Pennsylvani.; 1609-82. Philadelphia, 1850.

Hazard, Samuel, Register of Pennsylvania.

Henninghausen, L. P., The Redemptioners and the German Society of Maryland. Baltimore, 1888.

Hildreth, Richard, History of the United States. New York, 1851.

Historical Collection relating to Gwynedd (township), by H. M. Jenkins. Philadelphia, 1884.

Historical Collections of the State of Pennsylvania, by S. Day. Philadelphia, New Haven, 1843.

History of Bucks County (Pa.), W. W. H. Davis. Doylestown, Pa., 1876.

History of Chester County (Pa.), Futhey & Cope. Phila., 1881.

History of Delaware County, Geo. Smith. Philadelphia, 1862.

History of Montgomery County, T. W. Bean. Philadelphia, 1884.

History of Western Pennsylvania and the West, by I. D. Rupp. Harrisburg, Pittsburg, 1846.

History of Westmoreland County, G. D. Albert. Philadelphia, 1882.

Hurd, J. C., The Law of Freedom and Bondage in the United States, 2 v. Boston, 1858.

Journal of the House of Commons, vol. xvi. 1803.

Kalm, Peter, Travels into North America. London, 1772.

Kapp, Friederick, Immigration and the Commissioners of Immigration of the State of New York; appendix. New York, 1870.

Laws of the Commonwealth of Pennsylvania; 1700-1781; by A. J. Dallas. Philadelphia, 1791.

Laws of Maryland made since 1763. Annapolis, 1787.

Laws of Maryland, at large, by Thomas Bacon. Annapolis, 1765.

Laws of the State of New Jersey; revised by Paterson. New Brunswick, 1800.

Lecky, W. E. H., History of England in the 18th Century. New York, 1893.

Lewis, L., Original Land Titles in Philadelphia. Philadelphia, 1880.

Lodge, Henry C., A Short History of the English Colonies in America. New York, 1881.

Loeher, Franz, Geschichte und Zustände der Deutschen in Amerika. Cincinnati and Leipzig, 1874.

Lord, Eleanor L., Industrial Experiments in the British Colonies of North America; Johns Hopkins Univ. Studies. Baltimore, 1898.

Martin, J. H. History of Chester County (Pa.). Philadelphia, 1877.

Maryland Archives, Proceedings and Acts of the Assembly; 1637-1692; 3 v. Baltimore, 1883-94.

Maryland Archives, Proceedings of the Provincial Council; 1636-1687; 2 v. Baltimore, 1885-87.

Maryland Archives, Judicial and Testamentary Business of the Provincial Court; 1649-57. Baltimore, 1891.

Memoirs of the Historical Society of Pennsylvania, vol. i. Philadelphia, 1826.

Mittleberger, G., Journey to Pennsylvania, 1750; trans. by C. T. Eben. Philadelphia, 1898.

Egle, N. H., Names of Foreigners who took the Oath of Allegiance to the Province and State of Pennsylvania. Harrisburg, 1890.

New England Magazine, (L. H. Harley), 15:145.

Neill, Edward D., Terra Mariae. Philadelphia, 1869.

New Jersey, Archives of the State of, 1st series, ed. by W. A. Whitehead. Newark, 1880.

Palatine or German Immigration to New York and Pennsylvania, by S. H. Cobb, in Wyoming Hist. and Geological Soc. Wilkes Barre, 1897.

Pennypacker, The Settlement of Germantown. Phila., 1899.

Pennsylvania German Society Proceedings. Lancaster, 1897.

Pennsylvania Magazine of History and Biography, vols. iv, xviii and xx. Philadelphia, 1896.

Pennsylvania Archives, ed. by S. Hazard, vols. ii, iv and viii.

Pennsylvania Gazette, in Hist. Soc. of Pa.

Pennsylvania, Minutes of the Provincial Council of, i, iii, iv, vi, vii, viii, ix, x, xi. (Colonial Records).

Pennsylvania Packet, Hist. Soc. of Pa.

Prendergast, J. P., The Cromwellian Settlement of Ireland. London, 1870.

Proud, Robert, History of Pennsylvania, v. 2. Philadelphia. 1798.

Raynal, Abbé, History, Settlement and Trade of Europeans in the East and West Indies. London, 1783.

Record of the Court at Upland in Pennsylvania, etc. Phila., 1860.

Records of New Amsterdam, 1653-74. New York, 1897.

Reed, John, An Explanation of the City and Liberties of Philadelphia (1774); reprinted. Philadelphia, 1846.

Registry of Redemptioners; 1785-1831; MSS. in Hist. Soc. of Pa.

Relation of Maryland, A, 1635; reprint. New York, 1865.

Rupp, I. D., Collection of Thirty Thousand Names of Immigrants in Pennsylvania, 1727-76. Philadelphia, 1876.

Rupp, I. D., History and Topography of Dauphin, Cumberland, Franklin, etc., Counties. Lancaster, 1846.

Rupp, I. D., History of Northampton, Lehigh, etc., Counties. Harrisburg, 1845.

Rupp, I. D., History of Northumberland, Huntington, etc., Counties. Lancaster, 1847.

Rush, Benjamin, Manners of German Inhabitants of Pennsylvania. Philadelphia, 1875.

Sachse, J. F., The German Pietists of Provincial Pennsylvania. Philadelphia, 1895.

Salmon, Lucy M., Domestic Service. New York, 1897.

Scharf, J. T., History of Maryland. Baltimore, 1857.

Scharf, J. T., Chronicles of Baltimore. Baltimore, 1874.

Scharf and Wescott, A History of Philadelphia. Phila., 1884.

Schlözer, August, Briefwechsel; erster Theil, Heft i-vi. Göttingen, 1777.

Scott, George, The Model of the Government of the Province of New Jersey in America. (1685); reprinted in Collection of New Jersey Hist. Soc. i. Newark, 1874.

Seidensticker, Oswald, Geschichte der Deutschen Gesellschaft von Pennsylvanien. Phila., 1874.

Smith, Samuel, The History of the Colony of Nova Caesaria or New Jersey. Phila., 1765.

Stevens, W. B., History of Georgia. New York, 1847.

Statutes at Large (English), vols. v, vi, and vii. London, 1764.

Statutes at Large of Pennsylvania. 1896.

Sutcliff, Robt., Travels in some parts of America, 1804-6. London, 1811.

Sypher, J. R., History of Pennsylvania. Phila., 1868.

Thurloe, John, Collection of State Papers; ed. by Birch, 7 v. London, 1853.

Verney Family Papers; ed. by John Bruce. London, 1853.

Walsh, Robert, An Appeal from the Judgment of Great Britain. Phila., 1819.

Watson, John F., Annals of Philadelphia and Pennsylvania. Phila., 1857-79.

Whitehead, W. A., Contributions to the earlier history of Perth Amboy. New York, 1855.

Williamson, Peter, Life and Adventures of. Liverpool, 1807.

INDEX.

Supplement to the YALE REVIEW, Vol. X, No. 2, August, 1901.

REDEMPTIONERS

AND

INDENTURED SERVANTS

IN THE

COLONY AND COMMONWEALTH

OF

PENNSYLVANIA

BY

KARL FREDERICK GEISER, Ph.D.

Professor of Political Science, Iowa State Normal School. Sometime Assistant in American History, Yale University.

THE TUTTLE, MOREHOUSE & TAYLOR CO.,
125 TEMPLE STREET, NEW HAVEN, CONN.

PLEASE RETURN TO
ALDERMAN LIBRARY

DUE

12/13/89

12-12-9

DUE

Lightning Source UK Ltd.
Milton Keynes UK
UKHW021943290719
347034UK00008B/175/P

9 780342 153312